to Carole:
Happy ♥
coo
I Love you and
want you
Every Woman's Guide to

$\mathcal{R}$omance in Paris

with
me.
Love,
Love

Caroline O'Connell

AVERY PUBLISHING GROUP INC.
Garden City Park, New York

Cover Design: Rudy Shur and Martin Hochberg.
Front Cover Photo: Carlos Spaventa.
Back Cover Photo: Alexis Garfield; Makeup by Paula Begoun.
In-House Editor: Joanne Abrams.

Library of Congress Cataloging-in-Publication Data

O'Connell, Caroline.
    Every woman's guide to romance in Paris / Caroline O'Connell.
      p. cm.
    Includes bibliographical references (p.) and index.
    ISBN 0-89529-437-0
    1. Paris (France)—Description—Guide-books. 2. Women—
Travel—France—Paris—Guide-books. I. Title.
DC708.025 1992
914.4'3604839—dc20   91-25589
                                              CIP

Printed in the United States of America

10 9 8 7 6 5 4 3 2 1

Contents

For Warren Bennis and Jean Berchon,
two very dear men
who have each had a profound effect on my life.
Merci pour tout.

CREDITS

Excerpts

The inset on page 28 is reprinted with the permission of Argonne National Laboratory.

The excerpts on pages 52, 53, 54, and 116 are from *French Chic* by Susan Sommers. Copyright © 1988 by Susan Sommers. Reprinted by permission of Villard Books, a division of Random House, Inc.

The excerpts on page 64 are from "The Thoroughly Modern Mistress" by Letitia Jett-Guichard, *Avenue*, January 1989. Reprinted with permission.

The excerpt on page 71 is reprinted from *Paris* by John Russell. Printed in 1983 by Harry N. Abrams, Inc., New York. All rights reserved. Reprint permission granted by the publisher.

The excerpts on page 84 and 100 are from *The Food Lover's Guide to Paris* © 1984, 1988 Patricia Wells. Reprinted by permission of Workman Publishing Company. All rights reserved.

The excerpt on page 107 is reprinted with permission by *European Travel & Life*. Copyright © 1987 News America Publishing Incorporated.

The excerpt on page 123 is from *Pierre Deux's French Country: A Style and Source Book* by Pierre Moulin, Pierre Le Vec, and Linda Dannenberg, edited by Nancy Norogrod. Copyright © 1984. Published by Clarkson N. Potter, Inc. Reprinted with permission of the publisher.

The excerpt on page 137 is reprinted from "Parisian Parks Are Where to Find French Showing Their True Colors," by Sam Hall Kaplan, *Los Angeles Times*, March 4, 1990. Copyright, 1990, Los Angeles Times. Reprinted by permission.

The excerpt on page 147 is from *Monet's Years at Giverny: Beyond Impressionism* by Philippe de Montebello, published by Harry N. Abrams, Inc., New York, 1978. Copyright © 1978 by the Metropolitan Museum of Art. All rights reserved.

The excerpt on page 149 is reprinted from "Footloose in Honfleur," by Beverly Beyer and Ed Rabey, *Los Angeles Times*, November 3, 1985. Reprinted with permission.

The excerpt on page 150 is reprinted from *France at Its Best* by Robert S. Kane. Published by Passport Books/NTC Publishing Group, 4255 West Touhy Avenue, Lincolnwood, IL 60646. Reprinted with permission of the publisher.

Photos

S. de Bourgies, Chic Promenade: page 119.

Hotel de Saint-Germain: page 13.

Moët and Chandon: pages 143 and 145.

Caroline O'Connell: pages 44, 51, 106, 111, 122, 142, and 146.

Frederic Reglain: pages 8, 12, 16, 26, 33, 39, 38, 49, 54, 56, 62, 73, 74, 75, 80, 82, 83, 92, 99, 100, 101, 102, 104, 113, 118, 125, 129, 133, 135, 136, 137, 141, 147, 148, 155, 157, 159.

Acknowledgements

I am grateful to many people for their encouragement and support over the many years it took to prepare this guide. Without them, this effort would not have been possible.

Liza Garfield and Leigh Reynolds are two very special friends whom I've had the good fortune to know for twenty years and the good luck to have had as traveling companions in Paris.

Sherry Robb, an ace literary agent, was the first person in publishing who believed in this project and showed me the steps to get started.

Rudy Shur and Joanne Abrams, my publisher and editor respectively, have provided wonderful guidance and painstaking editorial assistance.

Claire and Richard O'Connell, my loving parents, have always believed I could do anything I set my mind to and have always encouraged me to reach for my dreams.

Claire Merrill, my grandmother, was an elegant, special woman who had a deep, early influence on my sense of femininity and the finer things life has to offer.

Holly Hein and Orrin Hein, two dear friends, shared their expertise and gave me a base of operations in their lovely Paris apartment.

Frederic Reglain, Carlos Spaventa, and Peggy Ganong are my two Paris-based photographers and assistant. Their counsel, artistic contribution, and hard work were invaluable. And Shaena Engle provided much-needed support by retyping drafts and offering helpful suggestions.

Mille merci to Jean Berchon, Régis Bulot, Remy Camoin, and Patrick Terrail for their French expertise and lasting friendship. Also, thanks to Jerome Litt and James Rosenfield.

And finally, my three cats—Buttercup, Bello, and Tuffy—have been a constant source of joy as I struggled through each draft. A writer couldn't have three more devoted and loving felines.

Preface

My love affair with Paris began on my first trip there ten years ago. I was totally unprepared for the beauty, elegance, and excitement of the city. It was unlike anything I'd ever experienced. There were lively cafés and mouth-watering *pâtisseries* (bake shops) on every block. The shopping and dining were *très elegant*. The sites and museums conjured up images of a civilization that has been influencing the rest of the world for many centuries.

That first visit and subsequent trips to Paris served as a sort of finishing school for me by enlarging my knowledge of fashion, cuisine, art, language, and history. The tastes I've developed and customs I've adopted enhance my life every day.

I had not realized such a special, different world existed, and vowed to capture the essence and "bottle it" for my friends so that they could share in the same joys and insights. This guidebook is the culmination of my efforts.

There are many reasons for my decision to focus on romance in Paris. First, I don't know of a more romantic city that can offer so much for you and your amour to enjoy *ensemble* (together)—candlelit dinners in gourmet restaurants, beautiful gardens to stroll through arm-in-arm, fashionable boutiques to indulge your every whim, and, of course, fascinating monuments at every turn. Second, I think women are especially appreciated in Paris. As members of the "fairer sex," we can take advantage of many opportunities to be pampered—luxurious beauty salons, cozy hideaways for afternoon tea, and specialty stores devoted to lingerie, perfume, and *la maison*, the house. Third, Frenchmen are *très gallant* and charming. And, if you're of a mind to be swept off your feet, they can be very accommodating.

I have found that the more you are able to immerse yourself in the French culture and spend time around Parisians, the richer a trip you'll experience. For this reason, I chose to concentrate on places and activities in the heart of the city. The major sights and shops are all within a short walk, and you won't spend inordinate amounts of time traveling to a store on the outskirts of town. I recommend steering clear of major thoroughfares, like the Champs-Elysées, because they have become too commercial and don't reflect the romance of Paris. Instead, I suggest you explore some of the charming neighborhoods, like the island of Ile Saint-Louis and the area around Saint-Germain-des-Prés.

The format of this guide follows the logical progression of your trip, starting with preparation and travel arrangements. Every important travel category has been included—hotels, restaurants, museums and sites, and stores—all with an emphasis on the French culture. For example, although Paris has many good ethnic restaurants, like Italian and Chinese, this guide focuses on restaurants devoted to French cuisine. In addition, there are many features not found in other Paris guidebooks: special mentions of romantic hideaways; a chapter on Frenchmen and how to meet them; listings of beauty salons, exercise clubs, sporting events, and day trips to the French countryside; and explanations of French customs. To further help you savor the French experience, many French words and phrases have been sprinkled throughout the text in italics, with definitions immediately following. For easy reference, all of these terms have been listed again in a glossary at the end of the book.

I started work on this book a half-dozen years ago and have spent many months in Paris investigating possible listings, deciding what to include, and studying the French way of life. All the listings have been double-checked, and I paid particular attention to the hotels and restaurants. This guide would not have been possible without the assistance of a number of Parisian friends who contributed their time and expertise, explaining various aspects of French culture and cluing me in on those places that are quintessentially Parisian. I also benefited from the generosity of a number of American women who shared their experiences and filled out questionnaires. There are many books on France that I found invaluable, and they are included in a Suggested Reading List at the end of this guide.

Several criteria were used to select the listings. I focused on the three *arrondissements* (neighborhoods) that adjoin each other in the center of Paris; there, the main attractions are concentrated and you'll get the full Parisian experience the moment you step foot outside your hotel. For the most part, I tried to include places that are popular with the French so that you'll be able to get a deeper sense of *la vie Parisienne*. Then I looked for places that have charm and are rewarding experiences; many of the hotels and museums in this guide are smaller and "off the beaten track." Every category—hotels, for instance—contains some moderate-price and budget listings when possible.

Each listing includes the name, address, phone, *arrondissement* (region of Paris), métro stop (subway), and credit cards accepted. The credit card abbreviations are as follows: American Express—AE, MasterCard—MC, and Visa—V. When applicable, the cost is listed in French francs; often the dollar conversion is included. The exchange rate at the time of this writing is between 5 and 6 francs per dollar. To calculate the dollar amount, I divided the franc amount by 5 to be on the conservative side, so prices might be somewhat lower than the dollar amounts listed. All information was reverified right before printing to make this accurate and up-to-date.

The heart ♥ rating throughout the guide highlights my favorites in each category. In the case of hotels and restaurants, the heart rating indicates those places with an especially warm, cozy, romantic ambience. You'll find that every place listed is enchanting and opens another door for your personal dream trip come true.

From the moment you arrive, Paris will embrace you.

Introduction

Paris changed my life, and it can change yours too! There are so many wonderful things to discover and experience. From *haute cuisine* and *haute couture* to lively sidewalk cafés and sophisticated nightclubs, it all seems so elegant and unattainable. But it's not. With the right attitude and some important guidelines, you can adapt to the Parisian lifestyle and have the time of your life.

The City of Lights is truly a romantic wonderland. From the moment you arrive, you will be struck by the splendor and physical beauty: well-kept parks, soaring monuments like the Eiffel Tower and Place de la Concorde, fashionable boutiques on tree-lined boulevards, and street corners bustling with fruit stands and flower vendors. You will have the impression of being on a movie set, but the director will never yell "Cut." This is the real thing.

Everything in Paris seems geared to pampering women. The men are gallant and courteous. The shopping is unsurpassed. There are temptations for every imaginable interest—luxurious beauty salons, great restaurants, world-class museums, and jet-set discos. You name it, Paris has it.

Although this is a guide to romance, it is not meant only for women who will be traveling with a husband or boyfriend. Romance is everywhere in Paris, and its spirit can be savored and celebrated at any time and with anyone: during a candlelit dinner with the man you love; while walking alone through the enchanting Luxembourg Gardens; or with a girlfriend, sharing the fun and excitement of shopping for lacy lingerie and exotic perfumes.

This guide paves the way, so you can immerse yourself in the culture and day-to-day life of the Parisians around you. You may linger over an espresso with a friend at a popular outdoor café on the Left Bank, find bargains at the Clignancourt flea market, or spend a day at one of the neighboring parks or chateaux. The possibilities are endless.

1

You are certain to have many opportunities to make new acquaintances during your stay. I have found the French to be very friendly and hospitable. Parisian friends have thrown dinner parties in my honor and taken me out dancing till dawn. Shopkeepers have gone out of their way to explain nuances between our two cultures and show me ways of discerning top merchandise. In fact, this guide would not have been possible without the help and support of many French friends who have shared the intimate side of their Paris with me . . . and with you.

While you're discovering the French way of life, you'll realize that the French are fascinated by many aspects of the American culture. Our pop music is heard on the top radio stations and in restaurants; Levi jeans are the ultimate in style; and it is chic to label things in English. Best of all, American women are considered exotic in France, much the way French women are viewed in the States. So, you're off to a good start.

Once Paris has held you under her spell, the enchantment will linger on long after your visit. You may find yourself enjoying the cuisine at a local French restaurant, or spending an afternoon of pampering at a beauty salon, or splurging on an elegant suit. Or you may start planning your next trip to paradise—that's spelled P–A–R–I–S.

Bon voyage!

Caroline O'Connell

1. Les Preparatifs

Maximize Your Trip by Planning Ahead

Paris is beautiful year-round, but spring and fall are the best times to go. The weather is mild and delightful for strolling and exploring the city. Sidewalk cafés are bustling with customers soaking up the sun while enjoying an espresso and watching the passing street scene—a great show that goes on for hours.

In summertime it gets hotter, and the tourists almost outnumber the Parisians. Most French people take their month of vacation between mid-July and the end of August, and many stores and restaurants close for a few weeks at this time.

Whatever the season, Paris will charm you with her old-world elegance and beauty. There is so much to see and do. This chapter contains information on how to best prepare for your adventure and includes sections on deciding whether to travel with companions or solo, making travel reservations, obtaining a passport and traveler's insurance, exchanging money, asking friends for referrals, studying the language and culture, and packing.

Traveling With Companions or Solo

Should you go to Paris with a friend, with an amour, on a tour, or solo? Circumstances may dictate the answer, but, if given the choice, consider your options carefully. Strive for flexibility in your schedule to allow room for spontaneity. The best times are never planned.

Traveling With a Friend

Traveling with a girlfriend has many advantages. It is comforting to have a companion when you are in the midst of a foreign culture, and a female friend is a good confidante. I had a storybook trip with a vivacious girl-

3

friend who was quick to make new friends, especially with the photo of her five puppies. We were more adventurous as a pair, and our experiences were richer because we had someone to share and relive them with. We also shared fashion and beauty tips (and each other's clothes).

With a friend, you are safe going out at night to enjoy cafés, restaurants, and clubs. French custom is more conservative than ours, so a woman out alone at night is viewed as "easy prey," and is more apt to be hassled.

Since you will be together almost twenty-four hours a day, be sure you are compatible and have the same expectations. The Compatibility Test on page 5 will help you determine if this trip will make or break your friendship.

Traveling With an Amour

The romance of Paris is magical when shared with a loved one. There are charming romantic hotels, cozy candlelit restaurants, and beautiful walks to stroll arm-in-arm. When Parisians catch you in an embrace, they smile and nod their approval. Romance is *très populaire*—very popular. No matter how long you've been together, six months or fifty years, it will feel like your honeymoon.

Traveling on a Tour

The advantages of a tour are that it is economical, activities are planned for you, and you have traveling companions. Unfortunately, in most cases the disadvantages outweigh the advantages. You may find every minute scheduled with trips to the same popular sights that everyone else is standing in line to view. There is little room for individual pursuits or time to make new French friends.

If you are seriously considering a tour, here are some questions to ask:

- What is the cost? Does it include travel insurance, meals, museum fees, and transportation in Paris?
- What is the luxury level? Is the plane a large commercial carrier or a no-frills charter? What is the hotel rating; will you share a room with someone else; will you have a bath; and where is the hotel located?
- How many people will be in the group? Will there be mainly couples, or will there be other women with whom you can hook up?
- What is the daily itinerary? Will you be awakened early each morning for a full day of sightseeing, or will there be activities available that you can choose from, and, if so, will you pay individually for what you do?
- Will your money be refunded if the tour is canceled?

Compatibility Test

If you're thinking about traveling with a friend, you want to make sure that the two of you have the same goals and will be compatible. Remember that you'll be in close proximity with this person for up to twenty-four hours a day, especially if you plan to share a room. These five questions will help insure that this will be a dream you'll share a lifetime—instead of a nightmare you'd rather forget.

1. Do you have the same goals?
   - ☐ dancing every night
   - ☐ shopping up a storm
   - ☐ spending two full days at the Louvre Museum

2. Are you an early riser or a night owl?
   - ☐ wants to wake for an early morning jog
   - ☐ enjoys partying till dawn
   - ☐ must have an afternoon siesta

3. Do you have the same budget?
   - ☐ frugal
   - ☐ moderate to comfortable
   - ☐ money to burn

4. Are your temperaments similar?
   - ☐ must have every creature comfort
   - ☐ is spontaneous and serendipitous
   - ☐ is accustomed to making all the decisions

5. What is your fluency in French?
   - ☐ understands a few phrases, like *s'il vous plaît* and *merci beaucoup*
   - ☐ fluent, and impatient with those who aren't
   - ☐ helpless, and dependent on others to get around

Traveling Solo

Women who love the freedom of traveling solo are willing to sacrifice the security of companionship. Without a tour guide to filter your contact with the French people, you are bound to strike up conversations and make new acquaintances.

Once in Paris, if you desire to seek out other Americans, here are some places where you will find them:

- On English-speaking tours in museums or on the half-day bus tour of the city (see page 34).
- At your hotel. Check with the concierge.

- At the American Express Office, located near the Opéra (see page 63).
- At the American Church (see page 63).

Making Travel Reservations

Try to make your plans at least two to three months ahead, because some hotels and flights are fully booked well in advance. Your budget and comfort requirements will guide you to the best mode of travel. I try to economize on travel costs so that I can use the money saved to buy clothes, perfume, and presents.

If you don't already have an experienced travel agent, ask friends for a referral. A good travel agent will advise you on most aspects of your itinerary.

Making Plane Reservations

After consulting with your travel agent, you can do additional research by checking the travel section of your local newspaper for airline and tour-operator advertisements. Plane prices vary, depending on the time of year—summer is most expensive—and level of luxury. On my first few trips, I flew charter and saved hundreds of dollars. What was lacking in comfort was compensated for by the comraderie among the passengers and flight crew. Charters have that pioneer spirit!

Finding the Right Hotel

One of the wonderful things about Paris is that you can find charming, moderately priced hotels. You don't have to spend over $100 per night, as is the case in major American cities. Another difference is that bathrooms are not automatically included with all rooms. You need to specify if you want a bath (*bain*) or shower (*douche*).

The key consideration is location. You want to be in the heart of the city, where street life is bustling and Paris' historic sights and shops are within a short walk. Paris has twenty neighborhoods called *arrondissements*. Three *arrondissements*—the first (*premier*), sixth (*sixième*), and eighth (*huitième)*—border the Seine River and each other in the center of the city (*centre de la ville*). Most of the places suggested in this guide are concentrated in these three *arrondissements*. (See The Lay of the Land on page 10.)

HOTELS

When compiling the following list, I looked for hotels that were clean, charming, recognized by the French Tourist Office, and in attractive surroundings. The differences in price reflect the levels of luxury. Hotel rates have been expressed in both francs and dollars. When this guide went to print, the exchange rate was a little over 5 francs to the dollar. So, to determine the dollar amount, I divided the franc amount by 5. Of course, the exchange rate may be different when you plan your trip.

The heart ♥ rating indicates listings that have a romantic ambience.

Key to Hotel Listings
Deluxe—$200 and over
Expensive—$130–$200
Moderate—$75–$130
Bargain—Some rooms under $75
(Prices are per person, double occupancy)

AE—American Express
MC—Master Card
V—Visa

The Premier Arrondissement

The *premier* (first) *arrondissement* is the hallmark of luxury and elegance. Once the neighborhood of kings, it is now home to the Louvre Museum, Tuileries Gardens, Palais Royal, and the start of Rue St.-Honoré—a famous street lined with designer shops. There are many deluxe hotels, but you can find a few with reasonable prices.

DUMINY-VENDOME (EXPENSIVE)

This clean, modern hotel is situated in a fashionable neighborhood near Place Vendôme, the Tuileries Gardens, and my favorite tea salon, Angelina. The prices are reasonable for the *quartier* (area). The rooms are small.

3–5 Rue du Mont-Thabor
Phone: 42–60–32–80
1st *arrondissement*
Métro: Tuileries
Cards: AE, MC, V
Cost: 740–830 francs ($148–$166)

HOTEL DE LONDRES ET DE STOCKHOLM (MODERATE)

This is very quaint and charming, but there are many flights of stairs. Some of the single rooms are less expensive.

13 Rue St.-Roch
Phone: 42–60–15–62
1st *arrondissement*
Métro: Tuileries
Cards: MC, V
Cost: 500 francs ($100)

The Ritz Hotel.

HOTEL MEURICE (DELUXE)

This palatial hotel, facing the Tuileries Gardens, is so appealing that the Germans made it their headquarters during the World War II occupation. That stigma has passed. Today, guests are pampered, and the location is divine.

228 Rue de Rivoli
Phone: 42–60–38–60
1st *arrondissement*
Métro: Tuileries
Cards: AE, MC, V
Cost: 2,200–2,650
francs ($440–$530)

HOTEL MOLIERE (MODERATE)

The prices here are quite reasonable for lovely rooms with large bathrooms in a charming neighborhood near the Louvre and Palais Royal.

21 Rue Molière
Phone: 42–96–22–01
1st *arrondissement*
Métro: Palais-Royal
Cards: AE, MC, V
Cost: 470–580 francs
($94–$116)

HOTEL SAINT-ROCH (BARGAIN)

This is definitely a bargain price for the upscale neighborhood. The rooms are attractive and small.

25 Rue St.-Roch
Phone: 42–60–17–91
1st *arrondissement*
Métro: Tuileries
Cards: AE
Cost: 330–450 francs
($66–$90)

HOTEL SAINT-ROMAIN (MODERATE)

This is my sentimental favorite—the first Paris hotel I stayed in. At that time, it was listed in *Frommer's Guide to Europe on $20 a Day*. Yes, times have changed. The rooms are lovely, but the decor is modern.

5–7 Rue St.-Roch
Phone: 42–60–31–70
1st *arrondissement*
Métro: Tuileries
Cards: AE, MC, V
Cost: 590–695 francs
($118–$139)

RITZ HOTEL (DELUXE) ♥

If you are going to go deluxe, this is my number-one recommendation. The Ritz Hotel is the essence of everything Parisian—elegant, exciting, and with a fascinating history. If those walls could talk. . . .

15 Place Vendôme
Phone: 42–60–38–30
1st *arrondissement*
Métro: Concorde
Cards: AE, MC, V
Cost: 3,350–3,900
francs ($670–$780)

The Lay of the Land

Paris is divided into twenty numbered neighborhoods, called *arrondissements;* they start in the center and spiral outward to the city limits. Each *arrondissement* has its own distinctive flavor and appeal. The Seine River divides Paris in half and is crisscrossed by thirty-two bridges, or *ponts*. The northern half of the city, referred to as the *Rive Droite*, or Right Bank, has long been the stronghold of merchants and royalty. The Left Bank, or *Rive Gauche*, was first settled by intellectuals, writers, and artists, and it remains their home.

The *Plan de Paris* is an indispensable pocket mapbook that lists every street and address by *arrondissement*. It can be purchased at most newsstands and bookstores in Paris. Address numbers are determined by position relative to the Seine. Streets perpendicular to the Seine start their numbering at the river and move outward. Streets parallel to the Seine are numbered from east to west. One source of confusion is that addresses on opposite sides of the street do not necessarily correspond as they do in the States; for example, number 22 may be facing number 55 instead of number 23.

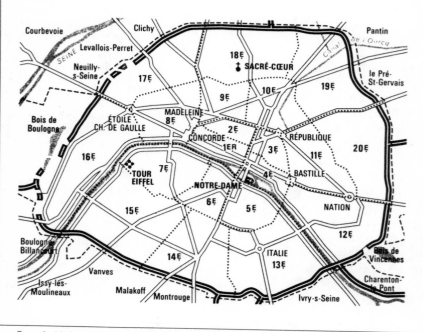

From the Michelin Paris Plan (1990 edition), Pneu Michelin, Services de Tourisme.

The Quatrième Arrondissement

Ile Saint-Louis, in the *quatrième* (fourth) *arrondissement*, is a tiny picturesque island in the middle of the Seine River. If you're looking for romance and charm, go no further. You will definitely feel you've stepped into an era in which time stands still. The main street, Rue St.-Louis-en-l'Ile, is overflowing with shops, cafés, and numerous ice cream stands. Notre Dame towers a few feet away on the adjoining island.

HOTEL DE LUTECE (MODERATE)

I'm not crazy about this hotel, but if the other three are booked *(complet)*, it's another option in a superb location.

65 Rue St.-Louis-en-l'Ile
Phone: 43–26–23–52
4th *arrondissement*
Métro: Pont-Marie
Cards: None
Cost: 650 francs ($130)

HOTEL DES DEUX-ILES (MODERATE)

The lobby is quaint, and the rooms are clean and pretty. But, if given the choice, I'd save $30 per night and stay in Hotel Saint-Louis (see listing below).

59 Rue St.-Louis-en-l'Ile
Phone: 43–26–13–35
4th *arrondissement*
Métro: Pont-Marie
Cards: None
Cost: 650 francs ($130)

HOTEL DU JEU DE PAUME (EXPENSIVE) ♥

This is my favorite hotel on the island. Everything is impeccable, comfortable, modern, private, and geared towards pampering the guests.

54 Rue St.-Louis-en-l'Ile
Phone: 43–26–14–18
4th *arrondissement*
Métro: Pont-Marie
Cards: AE, MC, V
Cost: 800–900 francs
($160–$180)

HOTEL SAINT-LOUIS (MODERATE)

This charming seventeenth-century hotel has lovely, small rooms. The owners obviously pay great attention to the little details that make all the difference.

75 Rue St.-Louis-en-l'Ile
Phone: 46–34–04–80
4th *arrondissement*
Métro: Pont-Marie
Cards: None
Cost: 490 francs ($98)

L'Hôtel.

The Sixième Arrondissement

The *sixième* (sixth) *arrondissement*, also known as Saint-Germain-des-Prés, is on the Left Bank, just across the Seine from the first *arrondissement*. Since the 1920s, this area has been renowned for the writers and artists who frequented the local cafés discussing art, religion, and politics late into the night. Visitors enjoy the legacy that remains while browsing through bookstores, admiring antique shops, and bargaining with the aspiring artists who sell their sketches on Boulevard St.-Germain. The hotels in the *sixième* reflect this creative, artistic ambience.

L'HOTEL (DELUXE)

Known as a favorite hideaway for celebrities and honeymooners, l'Hôtel's decor is a bit overdone—lots of velvet and dark colors. But, every room is different, and l'Hôtel is definitely a unique experience.

13 Rue des Beaux-Arts
Phone: 43–25–27–22
6th *arrondissement*
Métro: St.-Germain-des-Prés
Cards: AE, MC, V
Cost: 900–1,950 francs ($180–$390)

HOTEL D'ANGLETERRE (EXPENSIVE)

This is a lovely, small hotel surrounding a courtyard. Every room is different, and you can request one with a view of the garden. In times past, Ernest Hemingway lived here.

44 Rue Jacob
Phone: 42–60–34–72
6th *arrondissement*
Métro: St.-Germain-des-Prés
Cards: AE, MC, V
Cost: 650–900 francs ($130–$180)

HOTEL DE L'ABBAYE (EXPENSIVE)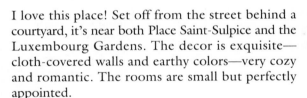

I love this place! Set off from the street behind a courtyard, it's near both Place Saint-Sulpice and the Luxembourg Gardens. The decor is exquisite— cloth-covered walls and earthy colors—very cozy and romantic. The rooms are small but perfectly appointed.

10 Rue Cassette
Phone: 45–44–38–11
6th *arrondissement*
Métro: St.-Sulpice
Cards: None
Cost: 690–1,200 francs
 ($138–$240)

HOTEL DE L'AVENIR (MODERATE)

The rooms are modern, not cozy, but clean and attractive, and the price is reasonable. The location is prime, a short walk from the spectacular Luxembourg Gardens.

65 Rue Madame
Phone: 45–48–84–54
6th *arrondissement*
Métro: St.-Placide
Cards: AE, MC, V
Cost: 406–476 francs
 ($81–$95)

HOTEL DE SAINT-GERMAIN (MODERATE)

The rooms are immaculate and decorated in country style. The location is excellent, in the heart of Saint-Germain-des-Prés.

50 Rue du Four
Phone: 45–48–91–64
6th *arrondissement*
Métro: St.-Sulpice or
 St.-Germain-des–Prés
Cards: AE, MC, V
Cost: 630–748 francs
 ($126–$150)

Hotel de Saint-Germain.

HOTEL DES MARRONIERS (MODERATE) ♥

A sure bet. I've recommended this hotel to many friends, and they've all given it rave reviews and are ready to return tomorrow. It is set off from the street, and there is a lovely garden in back. The decor is reminiscent of a country manor, and everything is spotless.

21 Rue Jacob
Phone: 43–25–30–60
6th *arrondissement*
Métro: St.-Germain-des-Prés
Cards: None
Cost: 540–600 francs ($108–$120)

HOTEL DES SAINTS-PERES
(MODERATE TO EXPENSIVE)

This is not my first choice for the neighborhood, but it is pretty and clean. The decor is modern.

65 Rue des Sts.-Pères
Phone: 45–44–50–00
6th *arrondissement*
Métro: St.-Germain-des-Prés
Cards: MC, V
Cost: 500–900 francs ($100–$180)

HOTEL RECAMIER (BARGAIN)

Some of the rooms are a bit shabby, but the location and price can't be beat. The least expensive rooms don't have a private bath; you go down the hall.

3–Bis Place St.-Sulpice
Phone: 43–26–04–89
6th *arrondissement*
Métro: St.-Sulpice
Cards: None
Cost: 320–850 francs ($64–$170)

HOTEL RELAIS CHRISTINE (DELUXE)

This former sixteenth century cloister is an ornate, gorgeously decorated mansion. The rooms overlook a garden and are equipped with all the amenities. My only small reservation is that the immediate neighborhood is run-down. A few blocks' walk will put you in charming surroundings.

3 Rue Christine
Phone: 43–26–71–80
6th *arrondissement*
Métro: Odéon
Cards: AE, MC, V
Cost: 1,100–2,100 francs ($220–$420)

HOTEL SAINT-GERMAIN-DES-PRES (EXPENSIVE)

The decor is a bit somber, but very luxurious. This hotel also comes highly recommended by friends, who return whenever they can. It's on a beautiful, small street surrounded by antique shops.

36 Rue Bonaparte
Phone: 43–26–00–19
6th *arrondissement*
Métro: St.-Germain-des-Prés
Cards: MC, V
Cost: 700-1,500 francs ($140–$300)

WELCOME HOTEL (MODERATE)

This is a rare find for the price. The rooms are small, but charming and tastefully done. One of the best fresh produce and flower markets is just outside. The whole neighborhood is wonderful—very chic, great shops, wonderful browsing.

66 Rue de Seine
Phone: 46–34–24–80
6th *arrondissement*
Métro: Odéon or
  St.-Germain-des-Prés
Cards: None
Cost: 455–475 francs
  ($91–$95)

The Huitième Arrondissement

The *huitième* (eighth) *arrondissement* is the business hub of Paris and is divided by the Champs-Elysées, a very wide boulevard. The French President's office, in the Elysée Palace, and the American Embassy are located at one end, near Place de la Concorde. The Arc de Triomphe, surrounded by the circular Place Charles-de-Gaulle, is at the other end. Elegant boutiques, luxurious hotels, and lively lunch spots abound. Due to the expensive surroundings, hotel rates start considerably higher than rates in other *arrondissements*.

I was not able to find inexpensive hotels in intimate surroundings in this area. But, if you want luxury and creature comforts and have money to burn, these hotels are quite a splurge. Otherwise, I recommend staying in the *arrondissements* mentioned earlier. (Note that the Pavillon Montaigne is less expensive than the others. It is clean and pretty, but, because it has modern decor, I can't classify it as quaint and charming.)

LE BRISTOL (DELUXE)

The Bristol is an elegant oasis in the heart of the city. The service is impeccable. The rooms are luxurious, and all the deluxe creature comforts are available, including a pool and sun deck.

112 Rue du Faubourg-
  St.-Honoré
Phone: 42–66–91–45
8th *arrondissement*
Métro: Champs-
  Elysées-Clémenceau
Cards: AE, MC, V
Cost: 2,900–3,500
  francs ($580–$700)

HOTEL DE CRILLON (DELUXE) ♥

Overlooking Place de la Concorde, the Crillon is a member of the prestigious Relais & Châteaux association of unique hotels known for their comfort and *bon accueil* (warm welcome).

10 Place de la Concorde
Phone: 42–65–24–24
8th *arrondissement*
Métro: Concorde
Cards: AE, MC, V
Cost: 3,150–3,500
  francs ($630–$700)

Le Bristol.

HOTEL DE LA TREMOILLE (DELUXE)

This hotel is less expensive than the other deluxe hotels in the area and just as appealing and comfortable.

14 Rue de la Trémoille
Phone: 47–23–34–20
8th *arrondissement*
Métro: Alma-Marceau
Cards: AE, MC, V
Cost: 1,960–2,650
   francs ($392–$530)

HOTEL GEORGE V (DELUXE)

The George V is another beautiful, formal, expensive hotel that caters to your every whim.

31 Avenue George-V
Phone: 47–23–54–00
8th *arrondissement*
Métro: Alma-Marceau
Cards: AE, MC, V
Cost: 2,580–2,870
   francs ($516–$574)

HOTEL PAVILLON MONTAIGNE (MODERATE)

As I mentioned earlier, this is very reasonably priced for the neighborhood. The rooms are clean and neat with modern decor. The street is quaint with many interesting shops.

34 Rue Jean-Mermoz
Phone: 43–59–54–29
8th *arrondissement*
Métro: Franklin-D.-
   Roosevelt
Cards: AE, MC, V
Cost: 450–480 francs
   ($90–$96)

HOTEL PLAZA-ATHENEE (DELUXE)

Situated on fashionable Avenue Montaigne, the Plaza-Athénée is surrounded by some of the top names in fashion—Christian Dior, Nina Ricci, Jean-Louis Scherrer, Emanuel Ungaro, and Valentino.

25 Avenue Montaigne
Phone: 47–23–78–33
8th *arrondissement*
Métro: Alma-Marceau
Cards: AE, MC, V
Cost: 2,650–4,180
   francs ($530–$836)

HOTEL SAN REGIS (DELUXE) ♥

I prefer this hotel to many of the others because it is smaller and not on a main thoroughfare. The Gault Millau guide labels it "one of the most chic and luxurious small Parisian hotels."

12 Rue Jean-Goujon
Phone: 43–59–41–90
8th *arrondissement*
Métro: Rond-Point des
   Champs-Elysées
Cards: AE, MC, V
Cost: 1,750–2,000
   francs ($350–$400)

Applying for Your Passport

As the form says, "Avoid the last minute rush." You should apply for your passport at least two months prior to departure. Passports are obtained through the United States Department of State Passport Agency, which has offices in every major city. If you have a few months' lead time, you can obtain the Application for Passport by Mail from your post office. You must have a "certified" birth certificate bearing the stamped seal (not a photocopy); another piece of personal identification, such as a driver's license; the filing fee; and two passport photos.

A French Visa used to be necessary, but that requirement was discontinued in 1989. If you want to get more information on French regulations for entry and extended stays, see the list of French tourist offices on page 19 for the office nearest you.

Traveler's Insurance

Check your medical insurance policy for coverage abroad. The American Hospital in Paris has full services, and the staff speaks English. The hospital requests immediate payment and sometimes accepts credit cards, depending on the procedure. It will be helpful if you have your insurance claim forms with you so they can be filled out by the hospital while you're there. You will then apply to your insurance company for reimbursement.

AMERICAN HOSPITAL
63 Boulevard Victor-Hugo (in Neuilly, a suburb of Paris)
Phone: 46–41–25–25

Theft insurance is covered in most renter's and homeowner's policies. If you are not already covered, there are companies that offer traveler's insurance, and it is well worth the extra few dollars. Purse snatching and lost luggage are all too common. I have spoken to many women who had purses grabbed from their hands, and I had a suitcase stolen from under my bed on a train while I slept. Insurance can mean the difference between having your trip spoiled or just suffering a minor inconvenience.

French Tourist Offices

The French government has four tourist offices in the United States set up to handle inquiries and provide detailed information for people planning trips to France. For example, if you want to stay in Paris longer than the ninety-day tourist visit allowed, the tourist office will explain the application procedure. Each office services a large region; the states it handles are listed in the left column.

There is also a (900) 990–0040 number (cost, 50 cents per minute), which I have found to be the most useful. You get through right away, rather than being left on hold; the operators can answer a wide range of questions; and the service offers free brochures on Paris and other areas of France.

States Served	Location of Office
CT, DC, DE, FL, GA, MA, MD, NC, NH, NJ, NY, PA, RI, SC, VA, VT, WV, Caribbean	New York: French Government Tourist Office 610 Fifth Avenue New York, NY 10020-2452 Phone: (212) 757–1125
IA, IL, IN, KS, KY, ME, MI, MN, MO, ND, NE, OH, SD, WI	Chicago: French Government Tourist Office 645 North Michigan Avenue Chicago, IL 60611 Phone: (312) 337–6301
AK, AL, LA, MS, OK, TN,TX	Dallas: French Government Tourist Office 2305 Cedar Springs Boulevard Dallas, TX 75201 Phone: (214) 720–4010
AR, AZ, CA, CO, HI, ID, MT, NM, NV, OR, UT, WA,	Los Angeles: French Government Tourist Office 9454 Wilshire Boulevard, Suite 303 Beverly Hills, CA 90212

Exchanging Money

Traveler's checks are an easy, safe way to carry currency. The advantage of traveler's checks over cash is that you are insured in case of theft. Remember to keep the receipt numbers and phone number in a separate place from the checks, so that you can call if the checks are stolen. American Express traveler's checks have about the best rate of exchange, but all major traveler's checks are accepted.

It is advisable to buy at least $50 to $75 worth of French francs before departing to use for small expenses upon arrival (taxi, phone calls, snacks), especially if you are arriving at night or on the weekend when the airport cashier is closed. In general, the banks in Paris will give the best rate of exchange.

Most stores and restaurants accept major credit cards, but some small, inexpensive hotels do not. Using credit cards is simpler than figuring out the amount in francs, and cards provide security in case of emergencies or unanticipated costs. I never leave home without my American Express and Visa cards. Some restaurants and shops do not accept American Express, so you will need a Visa or MasterCard as back-up.

In case of theft, I keep separate records of my cards at the hotel and with a friend in the States. One important note: American Express and some other major credit card companies tack on a one-percent fee for converting foreign charges into United States currency. This doesn't make much of a difference on small purchases, but can get costly if you're spending $1,000 (cost $10) or more.

The Importance of Referrals

This is one of the most important steps you can take to prepare for your trip. Paris comes alive when you are welcomed by a native. Speak to your friends and family beforehand, and try to get names of people you can contact when you arrive. I have developed many lasting friendships with French people I met through introductions.

On one occasion, I was traveling in Paris with a girlfriend who called a Frenchman she had met in a Los Angeles restaurant. He promptly invited us to afternoon tea with two of his associates. A few nights later, they held a dinner party in our honor and took us dancing—a perfect evening.

Studying the Language and Culture

You will find it much easier to navigate in Paris if you take the time to familiarize yourself with the French language. This doesn't mean that you need a degree in French literature, but it will make a world of difference if you are able to speak rudimentary French. When French visitors come to the United States, we expect them to speak our language. Why should it be any different when we go to their country?

Contrary to popular belief, the French are not critical of our accent when we speak their language. In fact, they find it charming, much the way we enjoy hearing French people speak English. They appreciate any effort you make, even if it's only to use simple phrases like *bonjour* (hello), *merci* (thank you), *excusez-moi* (excuse me), and *s'il vous plaît* (please). The French take great pride in their language, and even have a special group called the Académie Française that acts as a watchdog to preserve the integrity of the language.

There are numerous options for beginning your French studies. I recommend a class instead of a home-study cassette program. Many adult education programs offer French courses in the evening, and Alliance Française has branches in most major cities.

Another advantage of taking a French class is that you learn about the culture. Most courses include lessons on the history and modern-day traditions of France. When you arrive in Paris, the sights and sounds will be more familiar. Whatever your knowledge, Paris' charm and historical richness will intrigue you and instill the desire to learn more.

Many French phrases and their translations are included throughout this guide, and a complete glossary is provided on page 161. Two books with detailed information about French history and culture are the *American Express Pocket Guide to Paris* and the *Michelin Green Guide to Paris*.

Packing

Just as important as what you take is what you leave behind. The experts aren't kidding when they advise us to "pack light." If you don't, you'll wish you had. Some ways to lighten the load include using lightweight luggage and a rolling cart, mailing items home as you buy them, and leaving an outfit in your closet if you think you'll wear it only once.

I'm not of the school of thought that says, "All you need are comfortable, practical clothes." Paris is one of the most elegant cities in the world,

Sample Packing Check List

You'll feel more confident in Paris if you pack with an eye to both comfort and style. By using the following list as a guide and adapting it to fit your needs, you'll be able to dress well and avoid the burden of excess baggage.

Clothes

- [ ] two skirts
- [ ] two pairs slacks
- [ ] one pair jeans
- [ ] three blouses
- [ ] two sweaters

- [ ] two dresses
- [ ] two matching jackets or blazers
- [ ] one raincoat or heavier coat during winter
- [ ] exercise clothes (optional)

Lingerie (enough for five days, then hand wash)

- [ ] underwear
- [ ] slips
- [ ] bras and camisoles
- [ ] pantyhose and knee-high stockings

- [ ] socks
- [ ] T-shirts
- [ ] pajamas
- [ ] lightweight robe

Accessories

- [ ] two pairs pumps
- [ ] one pair tennis or running shoes
- [ ] one pair comfortable sandals (summer) or boots (winter)
- [ ] one daytime purse with compartments

- [ ] one evening purse
- [ ] belts
- [ ] scarves
- [ ] inexpensive jewelry
- [ ] watch
- [ ] gloves (during winter)
- [ ] sunglasses

Sundries
(in small watertight containers)

- [ ] hand and body lotion
- [ ] face cleansers and moisturizers
- [ ] shampoo and conditioner
- [ ] shower cap

- [ ] comb and brush
- [ ] hairpins and ties
- [ ] Vaseline petroleum jelly and lip gloss

Sundries

- [ ] deodorant
- [ ] cotton swabs and cotton balls
- [ ] toothbrush, toothpaste, and floss
- [ ] shaving needs
- [ ] tweezers and small pair scissors
- [ ] pocket tissues
- [ ] shoe polish
- [ ] small container of mild detergent or soap for washing lingerie
- [ ] nail polish and emery boards (don't pack polish remover, as it can spill; buy in Paris if needed)

Makeup

- [ ] foundation
- [ ] blush
- [ ] eye pencil, liner, shadow, and concealer
- [ ] mascara
- [ ] lipstick
- [ ] perfume (in nonaerosol container)

Medical

- [ ] aspirin or equivalent
- [ ] Band-Aid adhesive bandages
- [ ] prescription medications
- [ ] sanitary needs
- [ ] eye drops and extra pair of glasses or contact lenses
- [ ] sunscreen

Appliances/Miscellaneous

- [ ] portable hair dryer with *adapter plug and converter for French outlet, 220 volts*
- [ ] travel iron with *adapter plug and converter*
- [ ] non-electric travel alarm clock
- [ ] calculator (for converting currency)
- [ ] small sewing kit and safety pins
- [ ] Swiss knife (with wine corkscrew)
- [ ] camera and film
- [ ] travel address book
- [ ] writing materials and calendar
- [ ] umbrella (small, portable)

Don't Forget

- [ ] passport
- [ ] plane tickets
- [ ] itinerary
- [ ] traveler's checks
- [ ] credit cards

and the women dress very smartly. You will receive better service and will be treated with more respect if you are dressed for the part. It is true that how we look affects how we feel, as well as how others respond.

The first step is to go through your wardrobe. Using a three-color scheme (any primary color with black and white works), pick out the separates (skirts, pants, and blouses) that match and are the most flattering. Add a few dressy outfits for evening to wear to dinners, a party, or a nightclub.

The season will affect your choices. The temperature varies drastically from winter to summer, just as it does on our east coast, and the weather is always a bit unpredictable. Layer dressing is your safest bet. In wintertime, you will definitely need a warm coat and boots. Umbrellas are *de rigueur* year-round, because Paris enjoys summer showers.

The length of your stay may increase the amount of clothes you decide to pack, but don't go overboard. Ideally, you will have some outfits that don't wrinkle and can be hand washed. There are many dry cleaners, *nettoyage à sec* or *pressing*, but they're expensive and usually take a few days.

Shoes and purses are important to your overall look. Many young Americans make the mistake of traveling in running shoes with a backpack—not a glamorous sight. I wear running shoes when I plan to be on my feet for hours at a time, usually with other tourists at sightseeing spots like Versailles or the Louvre. I wear attractive pumps with a low heel when I'm among Parisians strolling elegant avenues, shopping in boutiques, or enjoying afternoon tea.

At least a week before your departure, decide what you will pack and make up a list. You may need to have that special dress dry-cleaned or your favorite shoes polished, so start planning early. The Sample Packing Check List on pages 22–23 may help you pack for your trip. Also refer to Caroline's Flying Tips on page 29 for items you'll want to carry with you on the plane.

Luggage

Luggage should be lightweight, but sturdy, with shoulder straps. Don't take one huge bag. Instead, break up the weight among a few pieces that are easier to carry. Pack an extra collapsible bag for new purchases. Label each bag inside and out with your name, address, and daytime phone number. A luggage rolling cart is a lifesaver and a "must have."

How to Pack

- Put everything in a staging area.
- Pack one small carry-on bag with essentials: money, traveler's checks, passport, plane tickets, documents, medication, some sundries, and a

change of clothes (in case your luggage ends up in another city).

- Stuff shoes with socks and stockings so they will hold their shape, and wrap them in plastic bags.
- Pack sundries in small plastic containers, and keep them in a separate compartment. You don't want to arrive and discover red nail polish on your favorite blouse. Ziploc freezer bags are great for this purpose.
- Set aside what you will wear on the flight. Dress comfortably, but not at the expense of style. The adventure starts at the airport, and you will definitely have the opportunity to make new acquaintances on the plane.

I used to leave my packing until the last minute, rationalizing that I might as well stay up all night so I could sleep on the plane. Invariably, it became a nightmare race against the clock, and I left important things behind. Now, I have learned to pack a day ahead, so I am rested, relaxed, and ready for the long trip.

My girlfriend, on the other hand, chose the night before our departure to make out her Last Will and Testament. "Odd," you might say. Well, she's terrified of flying and figured it was a good time to take stock and leave messages for her close friends and family members in case the plane didn't make it. Of course, I wasn't included in the will because she assumed we'd go down in a blaze of glory together.

The time you take to prepare for this adventure will help insure its success. Travel in itself is unpredictable enough without worrying about finding a hotel room or buying a French phrase book after you arrive. Anticipation and preparation are part of the fun. You'll realize Paris is no longer a faraway dream, but instead a close reality. And your romance with Paris will begin long before you step on the plane—and last long after you return.

Bon voyage!

13'20	FU	5413	AGEN	BERGERAC	14'50
13'30	IT	5845	NICE		14'55
13'30	IT	5243	PERPIGNAN		15'15
13'40	IT	5403	BIARRITZ		15'15
13'45	IT	5821	BREST		15'25
13'55	IT	5811	MULHOUS-BAL		15'35
13'55	IT	5743	GRENOBLE		15'45

MINUTES AVANT LE DEPART   VOLS AIR INTER : HEURE D'EMBARQUEMENT 20 MINUTES AVANT LE DEPART

Charles de Gaulle Airport.

2. C'est la Belle Vie

You Arrive! How to Adapt

No matter how much time you have allotted for your stay in Paris, it won't be enough. *C'est la belle vie* means "It's the good life," and you will soon realize why this phrase is so popular. The French savor the simple things in life to the fullest: sipping an espresso at a sidewalk café while observing the passing scene; tasting the sweet delights of a corner *pâtisserie* (bake shop); or strolling through one of the many colorful *jardins* (gardens).

This chapter will take you from your departure to your arrival in Paris and through the first few days of adapting to French customs and your glorious new surroundings.

The Flight

Airlines recommend you arrive at the airport at least two hours before your flight departs. They do this for a reason. You can plan on encountering long lines, particularly on international flights with increased security precautions.

Once on the plane, you are in for a long flight, and your body will feel the effects of arriving in a distant time zone. There are many programs for beating "jet lag"—the term used to explain why you feel as though you have been run over by a steamroller and want to sleep for twenty-four hours.

The Argonne Regimen (see page 28) was developed to help prevent jet lag on long flights. Many diplomats follow this regimen so that they'll be able to work as soon as they reach a foreign destination. You probably won't be going into high-level negotiations, but it would be nice to be able to jump right into your trip with energy and a rested body.

The Argonne Regimen

Typical jet lag symptoms appear when your body clocks have to speed forward or turn back in adjusting to a new time zone. The key to a smooth adjustment is following a strict feast, fast, feast diet before you board your plane.

The first thing to do is pick a flight that departs as early as possible when flying east. Next, determine what breakfast time will be on the day of your arrival at your destination, not at home. Three days before the day of your flight, begin the feast, fast, feast cycle.

On feast days, to stimulate the body's active cycle, eat high-protein foods like eggs, high-protein cereals, steak, hamburgers, and nuts, for breakfast and lunch.

For supper, eat high-carbohydrate foods which stimulate sleep, such as pasta, potatoes, rice, and sweet desserts.

Fast days help deplete the liver's store of carbohydrates and prepare the body's clocks for resetting. On fast days, try to keep your calories down to 800. Eat fruit, light soups, skimpy salads, and unbuttered half-slices of bread.

During the three days before your flight, coffee, tea, and cola are permitted between 3 P.M. and 4:30 P.M. only.

- *Day 3, prior to flight*: feast
- *Day 2, prior to flight*: fast
- *Day 1, prior to flight*: feast
- *Day of flight*: fast
- *On the plane*: Don't watch the film, work, read, or drink an alcoholic beverage. Set your watch to local time for your destination. Rest or sleep until a half-hour before breakfast, local time. (Even if your watch says it's 3 A.M., if it's breakfast time at your destination, then it's breakfast time for you.)
- *Before breakfast*: Stretch, walk in the aisle (if you're still on the plane), read, work.
- *Breakfast*: Break your fast with a high-protein breakfast, but don't drink tea or coffee.
- *At your destination*: Keep "feasting." (A high-protein lunch and a high-carbohydrate supper.)

Reprinted with the permission of Argonne National Laboratory.

Most experts advise that you resist the temptation to sleep when you arrive. Instead, it's best to put your body right into the time frame of the city. For example, if you arrive in the morning, eat a hearty breakfast and start exploring your surroundings. Also, recent studies indicate that exposure to sunlight can help reduce the effects of jet lag. By evening, you should be tired enough to get a good night's sleep. If you nap during the day, your sleep may be fitful that night.

I've never been disciplined enough to follow the Argonne Regimen, but I do have some simple tips developed after numerous flights:

Caroline's Flying Tips

- Freshen up by brushing your teeth and applying a light cologne.
- Use chewing gum to keep your ears clear.
- Keep hand lotion and lip gloss in your purse to help counteract the dehydration caused by cabin pressure.
- For the same reason, drink lots of "flat" water and try to avoid alcoholic beverages and carbonated drinks, both of which can dry you out.
- Bring snacks to munch on (juice, nuts, muffins), so you can eat when you're hungry rather than waiting for the meal service.
- Dress in layers, so you can adjust to the temperature.
- Take off your shoes and put on socks. Your feet will swell due to the cabin pressure, and socks will be more comfortable than tight shoes.
- To help pass the time, bring a novel in the genre you love.
- Every few hours, walk around and stretch to increase your circulation. This may not seem necessary at the time, but it will make a big difference in your overall feeling of well-being.
- If you have trouble sleeping on planes, there are two items that may help: an inflatable neck rest that fits around your neck and holds your head in a comfortable position, and shades that go over your eyes and fasten around your head with an elastic band. Both can be purchased in most stores that carry travel accessories.

If you're of a mind to make new acquaintances, you will have ample time and opportunity. My girlfriend and I met a wonderful Frenchman on a flight from London to Paris. It was very choppy over the English Channel, and my friend clutched Alain's arm in terror. He was immediately taken with her and struck up a conversation to practice his English. We taxied into Paris together and met the next day for lunch.

Airport Transportation

Although cabs are easy to use, you may not want to spend upwards of $40 to reach your hotel. Fortunately, both airports serving Paris have excellent transportation services that run on a frequent basis.

Charles de Gaulle at Roissy

This airport is the farthest from Paris. Signs will direct you to the stop for the Air France bus that departs for Paris every fifteen minutes from 6:00 A.M. to 11:00 P.M., at a cost of 37 francs ($7). The bus makes two stops in Paris, at Etoile and at Porte-Maillot. Etoile is more centrally located. From either stop, you will need to catch a cab to reach your hotel.

Another bus, part of the RER train line, will take you to a nearby train station that has service into Paris. This is less costly, 29 francs ($6), but more difficult to maneuver, especially with heavy luggage. Note that you will need to keep your ticket to get through the exit turnstile.

You can use either service to return to the airport. The RER train stops at two métro stations, Luxembourg and Gare du Nord, on the way back. Another bus company departs from Porte Maillot (a métro stop on the Pont de Neuilly—Château de Vincennes line) every fifteen minutes.

Orly

The Air France bus departs every twelve minutes and makes two stops in Paris, at Montparnasse and at Invalides. The cost is 30 francs ($6).

You can return to Orly on the Air France bus, or you can catch a train at Gare d'Austerlitz or a bus at the Invalides Air Terminal.

Finding Transportation to Your Hotel

There are many modes of transportation from the airport to your hotel. The easiest, but most expensive, is a cab. Paris has taxi lines that are similar to those in our airports. If you don't speak French, simply write your hotel name, address, and *arrondissement* (region of Paris) on a card, and show it to the cab driver. Or, you can use a very good bus service, run by Air France, that will take you into central Paris. The inset on Airport Transportation, above, describes various transportation services, explains how to use them, and lists the approximate cost of each one. For more information on transportation in Paris, see pages 35–39.

Arriving at Your Hotel

If you haven't reserved a hotel room in advance, the tourist center on the Champs-Elysées will help you find accommodations for a small fee.

Once you arrive at your hotel, make sure the room is what you requested. Many times, Europeans confuse the bed sizes (they frequently use twin-size beds), or fail to realize that most Americans expect private baths. Tipping is the same as in the States—tip the bellhop for bringing up your luggage, and leave a tip for the maid on your pillow when you check out.

OFFICE DE TOURISME DE PARIS
127 Avenue des Champs-Elysées
Phone: 47–23–61–72
8th *arrondissement*
Métro: Charles-de-Gaulle-Etoile
Open: Seven days a week, 9:00 A.M.– 8:00 P.M.

Befriend the concierge and desk personnel. They can be very helpful in answering questions and giving you advice about the week's events, sights of interest, and nearby shopping and dining. Also, pick up a few of the hotel's business cards so you will have the address and phone number with you at all times. These cards also come in handy when giving your Paris address to new French friends.

French Signs in Buildings

The floor numbers in French buildings are labeled differently from those in the United States. The ground floor is called *rez-de-chaussée*, and the first floor starts at the second level. This is similar to United States buildings that have a ground floor and then begin numbered floors.

Part of the culture shock you experience will be adapting to the French terms in buildings. Here are some translations to ease your transition and enable you to open doors and find the exit.

Dames	Ladies (for restroom)
Messieurs	Men (for restroom)
Ascenseur	Elevator
Escalier Roulant	Escalator
Escaliers	Stairs
Poussez	Push
Tirez	Pull
Sortie	Exit
Sortie de Secours	Emergency Exit
Interdit	Do Not Enter

Changing Money

Your hotel can change traveler's checks into French francs, but the rate of exchange will be higher than the banks'. Most banks post their rate of exchange in the window, so you'll be able to shop around for the best deal. An explanation of French currency and of how to translate French prices into dollar amounts is on page 33.

In times past, banks charged as much as a 9-percent commission for processing each transaction, so the French government passed a law to protect the consumer. It took effect in 1991 and dictates that the exchange price listed must include *all* handling fees.

Another new development is that there are now Automated Teller Machines (ATMs) in Paris affiliated with the PLUS and CIRRUS international networks. You insert your bank card, type in your PIN number, and receive French francs. The exchange rate is usually better than what you'll get with traveler's check exchanges and credit card purchases.

BANKS

You will find banks in all the major tourist and sightseeing areas. Normally, they are open Monday to Friday, but some close during lunch time. Here are a few suggestions:

AMERICAN EXPRESS

American Express's rate of exchange wasn't quite as good as the banks', and the line was longer. It is open seven days a week.

11 Rue Scribe
Phone: 47–77–77–07
9th *arrondissement*
Métro: Opéra

BANQUE NATIONALE DE PARIS

This bank is in gorgeous surroundings a few doors down from the Ritz Hotel. It caters to elegant businessmen.

7 Place Vendôme
Phone: 49–26–34–34
1st *arrondissement*
Métro: Concorde or
  Opéra

C.C.F. (on Left Bank)

This is a little hard to find—just off Boulevard St.-Germain, on a side street. The exchange tellers are found in a separate room.

4 Carrefour de l'Odéon
Phone: 43–25–38–17
6th *arrondissement*
Métro: Odéon

C.C.F. (on Right Bank)

In summer, June through September, C.C.F. is open seven days a week and caters to tourists. During other months, it is closed on Sundays.

117 Avenue des
  Champs-Elysées
Phone: 40–70–27–22
8th *arrondissement*
Métro: George-V

French Currency

At the time of this writing, the rate of exchange is between 5 and 6 francs to the dollar. I find it simplest to divide the franc amount by 5 to get an approximate dollar amount. For example, if the item is 300 francs, the cost is about $60. Naturally, when you go to Paris, you will adjust this formula according to the current exchange rate. A pocket calculator is invaluable if, like me, you're not a math whiz.

French franc notes come in various sizes; the larger the note, the higher the value. They start at 20-franc notes, worth about $4 (when you divide by 5). A 500-franc note is the most common large denomination in circulation (similar to our $100 bill).

The coins, known as *sous* or *ronds* in French jargon, start at a *centime* (100 equal 1 franc) and go as high as 10-franc coins.

Getting to Know Your Neighborhood

As you prepare to explore the immediate neighborhood around your hotel, make sure you have a good map. The front desk will probably have a sketchy one-page map of major boulevards, but I prefer the *Plan de Paris*, mentioned earlier. It is an excellent guide and covers *every* street.

Now you are ready to venture forth and discover the nearby boutiques, cafés, and historic sights. If this is your first trip, you will be overwhelmed by the beauty of your surroundings. If you don't speak French, you will also be overwhelmed by the challenge of speaking to others. Smile a lot, say *s'il vous plaît* (please) and *merci* (thank you), and you'll be off to a good start.

One way to make yourself at home in the neighborhood is to frequent a local café. If you stop by each day for your morning *café crème*, after the first few visits, you will be considered a regular and will be given better service. This will also give you a chance to observe the daily routine of other habitués and to make new acquaintances. It is better to become intimate with one café than to know many cafés fleetingly.

An excellent way to acquaint yourself with the layout and major landmarks of Paris is to take the half-day bus tour (see the inset below for information on the two biggest companies). This will help you understand where things are located in relationship to each other, and will give you a better idea of which areas you might want to explore in greater depth.

Paris Bus Tours

There are two major tour bus operators in Paris, both located in the first *arrondissement*. They offer a wide range of tours with tape-recorded English commentary. I recommend a short tour that highlights the main attractions; this will give you a better idea of what you'd like to revisit and explore in depth.

Both of the following companies offer a two-hour tour of Paris' top sights for 120 francs. They also conduct half-day and full-day tours of historic sights outside of Paris.

PARIS VISION
214 Rue de Rivoli
Phone: 42–60–30–01
1st *arrondissement*
Métro: Tuileries
Cards: AE, MC, V

CITYRAMA
4 Place des Pyramides
Phone: 42–60–30–14
1st *arrondissement*
Métro: Palais-Royal
Cards: AE, MC, V

Using Transportation in Paris

The Métro

Paris has a wonderful, efficient subway system called the métro. In central Paris, there are métro stops every few blocks (see page 36). If you're going to be using the métro more than a few times, it's cheaper to buy a *carnet*, ten tickets for 33 francs (approximately $6.50, or $.65 each).

The métro trains run every few minutes, and are by far the fastest way to travel around Paris. Major intersections, called *correspondances*, require walking a fair distance underground to catch connecting trains.

The métro is open from 5:30 A.M. to 1:00 A.M., seven days a week. Many Parisians have advised me that it's not safe for unescorted women to take the métro in the evening. For this reason, taxis will be your best bet after dark.

Buses

Buses are slower than the métro, but are great for sightseeing. I strongly recommend taking the serendipitous approach and just hopping on a bus going in the general direction in which you are headed. Some of the bus routes are recommended by the tourist office on the Champs-Elysées, and the tourist office provides maps and written commentary. This is much less expensive than the half-day bus tours mentioned earlier, and you will be riding with Parisians instead of other tourists. If you are particularly enchanted with one area, you can get off, walk around, and catch another bus on the same line later.

The Paris system of bus routes is divided into five zones. Maps of the system are normally posted on the backs of bus shelters. You use métro tickets for your fare. One ticket is valid for two zones. If you go a greater distance, you use additional tickets. When you enter the bus, you punch, or *oblitérer*, the ticket in the machine behind the driver. You then hold your ticket for the duration of the ride.

The Paris Métro System

The métro, which stops every few hundred yards, is probably the most convenient mode of public transportation in Paris. There are fifteen métro lines, or *lignes*. Each line is labeled by a number and the names of the stops at either end. For example, the métro line that runs along the Rue de Rivoli and the Champs-Elysées is called M1. Château de Vincennes—Pont de Neuilly. M1 stands for the number of the métro line; Château de Vincennes is the farthest stop on the eastern end of the line; and Pont de Neuilly is the farthest stop on the western end of the line. One of the métro lines, M6. Nation—Etoile-Charles-de-Gaulle, goes above ground over the Seine and has a beautiful view of the Eiffel Tower.

The following translations will help you navigate in the métro stations:

Poussez. Push (on door).

Tirez. Pull (on door).

Billet. One ticket.

Carnet. Ten tickets.

Sortie. Exit.

Correspondances. Connecting métro lines.

RER. Special express métro lines that go into the suburbs and make only a few stops in Paris.

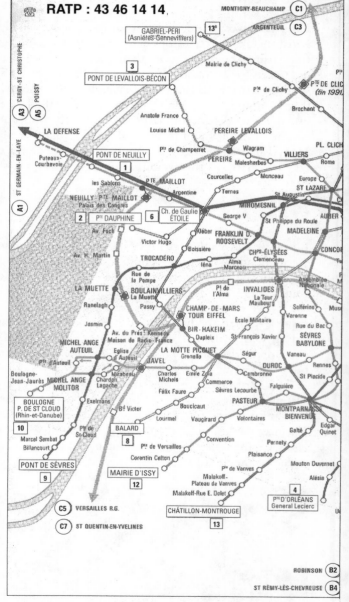

From the Michelin Paris Transports (1991 edition), Pneu Michelin, Services de Tourisme.

An Entrance to the Métro.

Taxis

Taxis are a more expensive mode of transportation than the métro, but they take you right to your destination, and you will learn about the city as you watch the passing scenery. The cost is about the same as the cost of taxis in major cities in the States. Tips are not included, so you should add 10 to 15 percent.

During the day, it is fairly easy to hail a cab on the street or to wait a few minutes at a taxi stand, or *tête de station*, where one is likely to show up. You can also phone one of the taxi companies to request a cab; just make sure you know your address, cross-street, and *arrondissement*. Two companies that serve Paris are Taxi Bleu, phone: 49–36–10–10; and G–7, phone: 47–39–47–39. Both understand English if you speak slowly.

To catch a cab for the airport, you can order a Mercedes taxi for the same price as—and sometimes a little less than—the others by calling Paris Taxi, phone: 60–17–84–84.

There are certain times when it is virtually impossible to catch a cab—at evening rush hour, during a heavy rain, and late at night—so don't assume that one will always be at your disposal.

Using the Telephone in Paris

If you don't speak French, you may encounter some difficulty when dealing with long-distance operators. The easiest method is to ask the hotel operator to place the call for you, but this will cost more than dialing direct. When away from your hotel, you'll be able to place calls from most post offices. (Post offices are listed on page 156.)

All of the phone numbers in Paris are composed of eight digits, beginning with a 4. The code for France is 33, and the code for Paris is 1. To call Paris direct from the United States, dial 011–33–1–Paris number. To call another region in France from Paris, dial 16, wait for a tone, and then dial the city code and number.

Key phone numbers are listed on page 41. You can also call Information, *Renseignements*, by dialing 12 and asking for an operator who speaks English.

Making Local Calls in Paris

The cost of a local call from a pay phone is one franc. Many pay phones do not accept coins, but require a phone credit card, or *télécarte*, that you buy at a *tabac* or post office. A 40-franc card buys you 50 francs worth of calls.

Even if you don't speak French, by mastering a few simple phrases, you should be able to contact the person you're trying to reach. The following are French phrases most commonly used over the phone:

You say,	"*Je voudrais parler à*" name of person.
	(I would like to speak to)
They respond,	"*De la part de qui?*"
	(Who is calling?)
You give your name.	
They respond,	"*Ne quittez pas*" or "*Un instant.*"
	(Hold on) (Just a minute)
Other phrases:	"*Entendu*"
	(Heard/understood)
	"*Il/elle est en ligne*"
	(He/she is on the line)
	"*Voulez–vous attendre?*"
	(Do you want to wait?)

Calling the United States from Paris

The least expensive time to call the United States is between 6:00 P.M. and 7:00 A.M. in the time zone you're calling.

To call direct through AT&T, dial 19, wait for a tone, and then dial 33–11. You will get an English-speaking operator.

To use MCI, dial 19, wait for a tone, and then dial 00–19. An operator will then come on the line to assist you.

To use Sprint, dial 19, wait for a tone, and then dial 00–33–00–87. The operator will come on the line.

Emergency Information

We all hope our trips will be trouble free, but if you do encounter an emergency situation, here are helpful phone numbers and addresses. They can all direct you to someone who speaks English.

AMERICAN CONSULATE
2 Rue St.-Florentin
Phone: 42–96–12–02
1st *arrondissement*

AMERICAN HOSPITAL
63 Boulevard Victor-Hugo
in Neuilly
Phone: 46–41–25–25

This hospital has full services, and the staff speaks English. For further details, see page 18.

LOST AND FOUND
36 Rue des Morillons
Phone: 45–31–14–80
15th *arrondissement*

The staff doesn't speak much English, and they prefer that you go in person to make a claim. They are open Monday through Friday, 8:30 A.M. to 5:00 P.M. The French term for "lost and found" is *objets trouvés*.

OFFICE DE TOURISME
127 Avenue des Champs-Elysées
Phone: 47–20–60–20
8th *arrondissement*

PHARMACIE (DRUG STORE)
84 Avenue des Champs-Elysées
Phone: 42–56–02–41
8th *arrondissement*

PHYSICIAN
Phone: 42–72–88–88

This twenty-four-hour service will send a physician to your hotel.

POLICE HEADQUARTERS
9 Boulevard du Palais
Phone: 17
4th *arrondissement*

UNITED STATES EMBASSY
2 Avenue Gabriel
Phone: 42–96–12–02
8th *arrondissement*

Understanding French Customs

The French are very polite and show a great deal of respect and formality when addressing each other, and their language reflects this custom. For example, the French have two methods of addressing people, the formal and the informal. While we say "you" in every situation, the same word in French can be spoken in two different ways—*vous* in the formal, and *tu* in the informal. The corresponding verbs have different endings, depending on the formality.

When French people meet, they speak in the formal until they become better acquainted—which can take years. And then they ask permission to speak in the informal. Young people address their elders in the formal, and some couples use the formal address their entire married lives.

This formality carries over into daily interactions. When a Frenchman buys something—a newspaper at the corner newsstand, for instance—he will preface his request with *s'il vous plaît* (if you please). We Americans tend to be more casual and direct in our communications, which can appear to be impolite to the French. I have found the best approach is to be friendly, courteous, and respectful, and to smile a lot. The French will respond in kind and will welcome your overtures.

Here are a few French customs to keep in mind:

- In most parks, it is *interdit* (forbidden) to sit on the grass. There are benches and chairs for those who wish to sit.
- When buying fresh fruit at a market or outdoor stand, it is customary to show the vendor what you want so that he or she can bag it for you. Don't touch the fruit yourself.
- Due to security measures, many stores, museums, and restaurants will ask to check your purse.

For all the differences between our two cultures, there are many similarities. If you put your best foot forward, you will be rewarded with a warm response. The salesman at a Charles Jourdan shoe boutique spent an hour giving my girlfriend and me valuable advice about ways of discerning top-quality merchandise. Another time, I went into a lingerie store to ask where I could buy a cat poster like the one in the store window, and the saleswoman took the poster down and gave it to me.

You are bound to return from Paris with your own wonderful examples of French *gentillesse* (kindness).

3. Les Fantaisies

Spoil Yourself and Discover the Secrets of French Femininity

One of the best ways to immerse yourself in Parisian life—and to recuperate from the transatlantic flight—is to spend a day among French women exploring the secrets of their femininity. French women have elevated the care, pampering, and display of their bodies to a fine art that is well worth studying and enjoying.

You might start at the beauty salon, where you will receive expert advice and treatments to nourish, beautify, and rejuvenate the body. The setting is luxurious and restful.

A visit to a French hair salon for a shampoo and blow dry is an ideal way to give yourself a lift and a great new look to kick off the first few days of your trip.

Lingerie stores will entice you with countless ways to lure that special someone in your life. The selection and quality of sexy lingerie in Paris is unsurpassed.

French perfume boutiques abound. You can choose a scent to "match your personality" and buy gifts for friends back home.

Sharing afternoon tea with a confidant is a fitting finale to your day of pampering and indulgence.

Armed with all this knowledge and allure, you should wear a badge to warn men that you're a *femme dangereuse!*

In this chapter, the heart rating ♥ indicates my favorite choices.

Guerlain Beauty Salon.

BEAUTY SALONS

There are a wide variety of treatments available in French beauty salons—massage, waxing, manicure and pedicure, facial, eyelash tint, makeup application, and more. (See page 46 for translations of beauty salon terms.) If this will be your first salon experience, a manicure would be a good choice. A professional makeup application is another way to add a sparkle to your look and give you fresh ideas for practice later. Many salons sell the products they use, so you can recreate that glamorous look whenever the mood and occasion arise.

Guerlain's Institut de Beauté is one of the oldest and most elegant in Paris. Completed in 1828, the building was one of the first erected on the Champs-Elysées. Guerlain—renowned for its classic methods, high-quality products, and discreet service—enjoys a stream of American clients, but the vast majority of its customers are well-to-do French women, sometimes many generations from the same family. The motto at Guerlain is *"La perfection de la tradition"* (the perfection of the tradition), and the salon emphasizes "luxury, calm, and voluptuousness."

The handful of top beauty salons in Paris offers a wide variety of treatments in beautiful settings amidst a parade of elegant French women. It is best to make a reservation well in advance. Costs vary from 170 francs ($34) for a manicure to 450 francs ($90) for a facial, and a 10-percent tip is optional. Most salons have English-speaking staff.

CARITA

Carita is a *très cher* salon for men and women on one of the most fashionable streets in Paris. After your session of pampering, you can window-shop at some very expensive stores.

11 Rue du Faubourg-St.-Honoré
Phone: 42–65–79–00
8th *arrondissement*
Métro: Concorde or Madeleine
Cards: AE, MC, V

GUERLAIN ♥

One of the oldest and most respected salons in Paris, Guerlain not only provides superb service, but does so in an atmosphere of luxury and elegance.

68 Avenue des Champs-Elysées
Phone: 43–59–31–10
8th *arrondissement*
Métro: Franklin-D.-Roosevelt
Cards: MC, V

INGRID MILLET

When you learn that Ingrid Millet has a caviar facial, you know this is the ultimate in extravagance and cost.

54 Rue du Faubourg-
 St.-Honoré
Phone: 42–66–66–20
8th *arrondissement*
Métro: Concorde or
 Madeleine
Cards: AE, MC, V

LANCOME

Lancôme's products are sold in the boutique on the ground floor, and the beauty salon is upstairs in subdued, tasteful surroundings. The *esthéticienne* will give you an analysis and detailed skin-care program.

29 Rue du Faubourg-
 St.-Honoré
Phone: 42–65–30–74
8th *arrondissement*
Métro: Concorde or
 Madeleine
Cards: AE, MC, V

Beauty Salon Terms and Costs

If, like me, you've experienced the frustration of trying to communicate in another language by waving your arms around and pointing, this list should simplify matters. You don't want to end up with a body massage when you went in for a manicure. The listed cost should give you an idea of what you can expect to pay for each treatment in one of the better salons.

ENGLISH	FRENCH	APPROXIMATE COST
Manicure	*Manucure*	170 francs
Pedicure	*La beauté des pieds*	245 francs *
Makeup application	*Maquillage*	350 francs
Body massage	*Modelage esthétique relaxant*	450 francs
Facial	*Beauté complète du visage*	450 francs
Eyelash curl	*Permanente de cils*	325 francs
Eyelash tint	*Teinture des cils*	200 francs

*This is the straight pedicure, not the *médicale*, which is more elaborate.

HAIR SALONS

French women strive for a natural, feminine look that requires minimal effort. They wear their hair in classic styles—clean cuts at chin or shoulder length, pulled back and tied with a bow, or worn short to frame the face. Hair accessories are used to add flair and to avoid spending inordinate amounts of time blow drying. Like many other aspects of appearance, this is something that's passed on from mother to daughter.

French hair salons differ widely from the elite and expensive to the smaller, less costly neighborhood salons. Passing a few hours in one of the top salons will give you the opportunity to rub shoulders with and observe a rare breed of French woman in a glamorous setting. (Translations of French hair terms can be found on page 48.) If you are following a tight budget, the neighborhood salons will do a very good job at half the price.

I suggest that you don't get carried away with a drastic new cut in the latest style. I made that mistake once and lived to regret it for months, until it grew out. I have also found that most French hair stylists aren't as good at coloring hair as their American counterparts.

A *shampooing* and *brushing*—equivalent to our blow drying—is a great way to pamper yourself at a cost of approximately $30. It is best to reserve in advance, but you can usually find a stylist to see you on the spot. Many hair salons are open Thursday evenings, and most are closed on Sundays and Mondays. Your hotel concierge should be able to recommend salons in the neighborhood. Here is a selection of the *plus populaire* and *plus cher* (most popular and most expensive) salons. Many of these salons have branches in parts of the city other than those listed below.

ALEXANDRE

Princess Diana's hairdresser, Richard Dalton, trained under Alexandre. Part of Alexandre's philosophy is to start with the basics and keep hair in good condition.

3 Avenue Matignon
Phone: 42–25–57–90
8th *arrondissement*
Métro: Franklin-D.-
  Roosevelt
Cards: MC, V

CARITA

Carita was mentioned earlier with beauty salons (see page 45). It also sells hair accessories—bows, clasps, etc.

11 Rue du Faubourg-
  St.-Honoré
Phone: 42–65–79–00
8th *arrondissement*
Métro: Concorde or
  Madeleine
Cards: AE, MC, V

Hair Salon Terms and Costs

While you don't have to be fluent in French to enjoy an afternoon in a French hair salon, it is important to be able to ask for what you want— and to avoid getting what you don't want. The following basic terms should help. Although I have included the word for "color," I recommend steering clear of color treatments because the French methods are often different from those used in the States.

ENGLISH	FRENCH	APPROXIMATE COST
Wash	*Shampooing*	30 francs
Cut	*Coupe*	150–180 francs
Blow Dry	*Brushing*	150 francs
Color	*Couleur*	Varies
Hair	*Cheveux*	Not applicable

CLAUDE MAXIME

This is one of the few successful salons founded by a woman, Claude Maxime, who started as a *coiffeur*. She has now branched out to other cities in France.

16 Rue de l'Abbaye
Phone: 43–29–74–20
8th *arrondissement*
Métro: St.-Germain-des-Prés
Cards: MC, V

JACQUES DESSANGE

Jacques Dessange is known for its good products.

37 Avenue Franklin-D.-Roosevelt
Phone: 43–59–33–97
8th *arrondissement*
Métro: Franklin-D.-Roosevelt
Cards: MC, V

JEAN-LOUIS DAVID

This salon is *très mode* (very chic). Customers look at photo samples and pick the stylist they like, and then the stylist suggests the cut he or she feels is most flattering. Be aware that you may not be able to sway the stylist's opinion.

47 Rue Pierre-Charron
Phone: 43–59–82–08
8th *arrondissement*
Métro: Franklin-D.-Roosevelt
Cards: MC, V

SOPHIE GATTO

This is a small salon off the Boulevard St.-Germain on a wonderful street lined with shops.

6 Rue du Dragon
Phone: 45–44–42–72
6th *arrondissement*
Métro: St.-Germain-des-Prés
Cards: MC, V

LINGERIE STORES

French women are notoriously seductive. They spend as much energy choosing what's underneath their clothes as they do on their outward appearance. They are also inventive and playful. A few years ago, it became sexy and *à la mode* for a French woman to wear men's boxer shorts instead of underwear. The Jockey Company has now come out with a line of women's underclothes very similar to its men's line.

According to French legend, Hermine Cadolle invented the brassiere in 1890 and liberated her clients from the corset. Ever since then, French women have been setting lingerie trends. Cadolle's *maison de lingerie* still exists on Rue Cambon and is run by Hermine's great-granddaughter, LeLorrain. The prestigious international clientele chooses from items in hand-sewn silk fabrics, ranging from a simple bra for $25 to a full-length

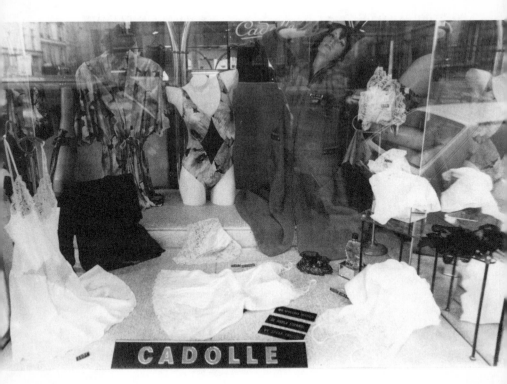

Alice Cadolle.

fitted nightgown for upwards of $400. I took the corset liberation one step further by purchasing an ivory silk camisole, which is *très confortable* (very comfortable).

One way to indulge in intimate apparel without spending a fortune is to buy silky-sheer French stockings. The Christian Dior store on Avenue Montaigne has a special boutique devoted to fine hosiery in imaginative variations (see page 108 for the address). French women are known for their attention to detail, and their preference for sheer stockings is one example of this subtlety. The one drawback is that sheer stockings are much more prone to snags and runs, but they are still an excellent way to get a flavor for the French sense of delicacy.

You will find one of the biggest selections of lingerie at the Galeries Lafayette department store, which carries many different designer labels. The ambience is not as intimate as that of most boutiques, but this is a good option if you are pressed for time. (Department stores are listed on page 112.)

ALICE CADOLLE
14 Rue Cambon
Phone: 42–60–94–94
1st *arrondissement*
Métro: Concorde
Cards: AE, MC, V

ANITA OGGIONI
19 Rue François-Premier
Phone: 47–20–74–76
8th *arrondissement*
Métro: Franklin-D.-Roosevelt
Cards: AE, MC, V

LES FOLIES D'ELODIE
56 Avenue Paul-Doumer
Phone: 45–04–93–57
16th *arrondissement*
Métro: Trocadéro
Cards: AE, MC, V

LES NUITS D'ELODIE ♥
1–Bis Avenue MacMahon
Phone: 42–67–68–95
16th *arrondissement*
Métro: Etoile
Cards: AE, MC, V

SABBIA ROSA
71-73 Rue des Sts.-Pères
Phone: 45–48–88–37
6th *arrondissement*
Métro: St.-Germain-des-Prés
Cards: AE, MC, V

The Parfumerie Fragonard

Perfume is of such importance to the French that there is a museum devoted to its origins and evolution. A visit to the Parfumerie Fragonard, located in an elegant townhouse from the period of Napoleon III, will help you "understand and appreciate the role of perfume in history and our society."

PARFUMERIE FRAGONARD
9 Rue Scribe
Phone:
47–42–04–56
9th *arrondissement*
Métro: Opéra
Cards: AE, MC, V

Perfume has its origins in the burning of incense during funerary rites; only later was scent applied to the body. The museum's collection of objects dates from 3000 B.C. up through the twentieth century. The range of perfume bottles exhibited shows the evolution of taste and fashion, as well as the development of ceramic art.

The museum is open Monday through Saturday, from 9:00 A.M. to 5:30 P.M., and admission is free. The gift shop offers a selection of scents and soaps at factory prices.

Perfume Flacons.

French Perfume

Perfume is a $3-billion industry in France, steeped in mystique and rich in history. Catherine de Medici founded the first perfume factory in Grasse, France in the sixteenth century. Grasse is still considered the perfume capital of the world, and students flock to this tiny town in the southern countryside to learn how to identify over 3,000 scents.

Coco Chanel was the first *couturière* to use her own name on a perfume when she launched Chanel No. 5 in 1923. Many other designers followed suit. Chanel No. 5 is still in big demand, and is regarded as the best-selling perfume of all time.

The renowned Guerlain line of perfumes has been in existence since the last century, when Pierre-François Guerlain created custom fragrances for members of European royalty. Today, at the Guerlain boutique (for address, see page 45), you are invited to select the perfume that best suits your personality. Each of the scents has distinctive characteristics and ascribed traits. Shalimar remains Guerlain's most popular fragrance. I chose L'Heure Bleue, created in 1912 "for women who are romantic, sensitive, refined, and feminine" (all qualities I'm aspiring to—at $112 per half-ounce). Guerlain's scents are sold only in their boutiques, not in other stores.

Perfumes are sold in many boutiques throughout Paris. Galeries Lafayette is the best place to find every scent—almost—under one roof. Most of the ground floor is devoted to perfume and beauty products. The salespeople speak English, and if you purchase over $240 in merchandise, you can fill out a form to be reimbursed for the luxury sales tax (see details on page 120). This is an excellent place to pick up small gifts like soaps, perfume atomizers, and bath oils.

"While lingerie is one secret weapon, perfume is another. Frenchwomen automatically link it to both seduction and fashion, and use it to create the right mood and atmosphere. Fragrance is integral to their sense of style and well-being. They select scents that are subtle and suggestive, apply them sparingly and then reapply them often throughout the day. Although her particular perfume is never the first thing you notice about a Frenchwoman, it is usually the last memory, lingering in the air long after she's gone."
—Susan Sommers
French Chic

Perfume is also sold at airport duty-free shops. This is fine for last-minute purchases, but airport shops don't always have the selection you find at stores in Paris.

DISCOUNT PERFUME BOUTIQUES

If you love to hunt for bargains, try the discount boutiques, which sell perfumes at a reduced price to foreign visitors. Vendors subtract the sales tax from the original price, rather than mailing you the reimbursement. Many of these stores are located next to each other on Rue Scribe in the 9th *arrondissement*, a block from Galeries Lafayette. They sell perfumes, makeup, some bath products, and a few gifts for men, like ties and belts. They all accept major credit cards and are closed on Sunday. Following are some of the best discount boutiques.

"Frenchwomen are faithful to their fragrance and use their personal scent as a signature, one with which they are associated and by which they are remembered. . . . Frenchwomen never drench themselves with perfume. They apply it in layers, so that the scent is gently released with their natural body movements. And they stick to the same scent for every form of fragrance used.

"They begin with scented soap and bubble bath or bath oil, followed by matching body lotion. They finish with eau de toilette for day, or perfume for night. They carry a small flacon in their handbags to refresh their fragrance every few hours."

—Susan Sommers
French Chic

BINGO
3 Rue Scribe
Phone: 47–42–98–62
9th *arrondissement*
Métro: Opéra
Cards: MC, V

CATHERINE
6 Rue de Castiglione
Phone: 42–60–81–49
1st *arrondissement*
Métro: Tuileries
Cards: MC, V

GLAMOUR OPERA
5 Rue Scribe
Phone: 47–42–00–30
9th *arrondissement*
Métro: Opéra
Cards: MC, V

HELENE DALE
253 Rue St.-Honoré
Phone: 42–61–80–23
1st *arrondissement*
Métro: Concorde (near
Rue de Cambon)
Cards: MC, V

MICHEL SWISS ♥
16 Rue de la Paix (on
the second floor)
Phone: 42–61–71–71
2nd *arrondissement*
Métro: Opéra
Cards: MC, V

PARIS LOOK
1 Rue Scribe
Phone: 42–66–59–81
9th *arrondissement*
Métro: Opéra
Cards: MC, V

Perfume Pointers

Shopping for a Scent

The French know that because fragrance is affected by body chemistry, a particular scent will not smell the same on any two people. They also know that scent in the bottle does not smell the same as it does on the skin, and that it must be tried on and worn for a while before making a decision about buying it. When you set out to sample the new scents, try a few French techniques:

- Try on a maximum of three scents at one session: the nose cannot differentiate between more.
- Shop for scent late in the day, when the sense of smell is sharpest.
- Apply fragrance to palms or insides of elbows, where perspiration and heat will help release it.
- Wait at least ten minutes before checking the scent to give it time to develop.

Where They Wear Fragrance

Both *eau de toilette* and perfume are applied at the pulse points so that the body's heat will help bring out the fragrance: behind the knees, between the thighs, the décolletage, throat, base of the throat, the insides of the wrists, elbows and behind the ears.

From *French Chic* by Susan Sommers. Copyrighted © 1988 by Susan Sommers. Reprinted by permission of Villard Books, a division of Random House, Inc.

AFTERNOON TEA SALONS

The perfect finale to your day of luxury and rejuvenation will be a break for afternoon tea at one of the popular tea salons. The French love to go out with friends and visit over a cup of tea while devouring a *pâtisserie*. It is a custom you will warm to immediately.

My favorite spot is Angelina on the Rue de Rivoli next to Place de la Concorde. Angelina has always been popular for afternoon rendezvous among models, journalists, and artists. Coco Chanel, Ginger Rogers, and Catherine Deneuve have all been devotees. Today, many elegant French women bring their well-behaved poodles, who sit demurely at their feet. The Belle Epoque decor sets the perfect mood to indulge.

Afternoon tea is an excellent way to enjoy the most luxurious, expensive hotels in Paris at a price much lower than what you would pay for lunch or dinner. Both the Ritz Hotel on Place Vendôme and the Plaza Athénée on Avenue Montaigne have afternoon tea service with harpist or pianist. They are more costly than other tearooms, but are well worth the price as they will allow you to catch a glimpse of the *crème de la crème* of Parisian society. The other salons cost around $10 for tea and dessert. All these salons are a big treat!

ANGELINA ♥

Angelina's specialties are the rich chestnut cream Mont Blanc and a very thick hot chocolate. The adjoining boutique has a beautiful selection of candies and souvenirs that make lovely gifts.

226 Rue de Rivoli
Phone: 42–60–82–00
1st *arrondissement*
Métro: Tuileries
Cards: AE, MC, V

CARETTE

Carette is best in warm weather, when you can sit at the tables outside and observe the passing scene at Place du Trocadéro.

4 Place du Trocadéro
Phone: 47–27–88–56
16th *arrondissement*
Métro: Trocadéro
Cards: None
Closed: Tuesdays

LADUREE

Located on the fashionable Rue Royale, Ladurée is usually very crowded because the pastries are renowned as some of the best in Paris. They also serve lunch.

16 Rue Royale
Phone: 42–60–21–79
8th *arrondissement*
Métro: Concorde
Cards: MC, V
Closed: Sundays

PLAZA ATHENEE

The setting is a luxurious sitting room with plush chairs in ornate surroundings. The cost is 40 francs for tea and 60 francs for dessert ($20).

25 Avenue Montaigne
Phone: 47–23–78–33
8th *arrondissement*
Métro: Franklin-D.
  Roosevelt
  or Alma-Marceau
Cards: AE, MC, V

RITZ HOTEL   ♥

The Ritz is my top choice for an unforgettable afternoon. In warm weather you are served outside on the terrace. The formal three-course "English Tea" costs 160 francs ($32).

5 Place Vendôme
Phone: 42–60–38–30
1st *arrondissement*
Métro: Concorde
Cards: AE, MC, V
Cost: 160 francs ($32)

TEA CADDY

This small, cozy hideaway near the Seine has wood paneling and tightly packed tables. Desserts, served on a platter, are just like those your grandmother baked. They serve both lunch and tea.

14 Rue St.-Julien-le-
  Pauvre
Phone: 43–54–15–56
5th *arrondissement*
Métro: St.-Michel or
  Maubert-Mutualité
Cards: None
Closed: Tuesdays

VERLET   ♥

This is one of my favorites—very small, wonderful aroma, and surrounded by French workers from the area taking their afternoon break. It also has a big variety of teas and coffees that you can buy to take home.

256 Rue St.-Honoré
Phone: 42–60–67–39
1st *arrondissement*
Métro: Palais-Royal
Cards: MC, V
Closed: Weekends

The salons, boutiques, and tearooms I've shared with you in this chapter are at the heart of what makes Paris such a special city for women. We are spoiled. We are pampered. We are admired for our feminine qualities. I know that these wonderful places have enhanced my appreciation for life's indulgences and I hope they will do the same for you.

4. Les Escapades

Meet the Man of Your Dreams

If you are traveling with a loved one, the romantic hideaways in Paris will be just the trick to keep the flames burning brightly. If you are on your own and in the mood to be swept off your feet, welcome to the City of Romance. The inspiration for writing this guide was the desire to convey that princess-for-a-day feeling you have when being appreciated and courted by Frenchmen in their capital. They are gallant. They are cultured. They are sexy. Frenchmen are *très romantique.*

American women are considered exotic in France, much the way French women are admired in the United States. American movies and music are an important part of the French culture, and, as a result, American women are viewed as glamorous and desirable. When Frenchmen learn I'm American, they approach with new interest and curiosity. I am constantly told how charming my American accent is when I speak French. The love affair between our two cultures is evident the moment you step off the plane.

Paris takes on a magical air when you are with an admiring Frenchman who acts as your guide as the two of you window-shop on elegant boulevards while discussing French fashion; stroll arm-in-arm through tree-lined parks; admire masterpieces in world-famous museums; enjoy a candlelit dinner; or dance the night away in an exclusive disco. The possibilities are endless. You may even experience a *coup de foudre,* or love at first sight; the literal translation is "flash of lightning."

In this chapter, you will learn about the special qualities Frenchmen possess, "hot" meeting spots, how to strike up a conversation (even if you don't speak his language), how to be selective and take precautions, and where to find romantic hideaways. The heart rating ♥ indicates my top recommendations. (Information on parks and sporting events, other excellent places to meet men, is in Chapter Nine.) Although the focus is on Frenchmen, romance in Paris can be with any nationality. You may meet a

dashing American, or you may share the excitement of exploring Paris with a traveler from another country. The city's lure is very seductive.
Vive la romance!

The Special Qualities That Frenchmen Possess

Spending time with a Frenchman will give you a new appreciation of your feminine qualities and a special outlook on the finer things life has to offer. Frenchmen love to spoil women, and will make every effort to sweep you off your feet. There are a number of traits that are characteristic of the Composite Frenchman. You probably won't find all of the following qualities in one man, but you are guaranteed to find many of them in the men you will meet.

- There is no better guide to Paris than a Frenchman. He is proud of his heritage and the rich French culture. He is well educated and will gladly take you to museums and sights and explain their history.
- A Frenchman is very gallant, and his *courtoisie* (courtesy) is inbred. Be prepared to be treated like a lady. The Frenchman will open every door and pull out every chair. Your wish will be his command.
- Sophistication comes naturally to the Frenchman. He speaks more than one language—including English (which is helpful for us). He is well traveled and enjoys sports and classical music. He is a connoisseur of good food and great wine, and you will be introduced in grand style to the good life, *la belle vie*.
- Your French suitor will compliment you on your best assets and make you feel very attractive. He is handsome in a sexy, Latin way, and he prides himself on his appearance. He looks as if he stepped off the pages of a men's fashion magazine. Every detail is in place.
- There is a tug-at-your-heart, poetic, romantic quality the Frenchman possesses that can easily win you over. He might bring you flowers or murmur adoring French phrases. Or he might cherish you by sharing his Paris. (Romantic French Phrases that are *très poétique* are on the following page.)

Romantic French Phrases

Remember that poetic, tug-at-your-heartstrings quality referred to in my description of the Composite Frenchman (see page 58)? I wasn't kidding. Would you believe these *très romantique* French phrases have all been murmured to me in utter seriousness—and romantic earnestness?

Je me jette à vos pieds.	I throw myself at your feet.
Je te bois des yeux.	I drink you with my eyes.
J'ai envie de te caresser.	I have the desire to caress you.
Tu me fais craquer.	You shatter my heart.
C'est long sans toi.	The time passes slowly without you.
Tu es rayonnante.	You are radiant.
Je t'embrasse partout, partout.	I kiss you all over, all over.
Je ne peux vivre sans toi.	I can't live without you.
Nous sommes faits pour nous entendre.	We are made to be together.
Tu es belle. Tu es belle.	You are beautiful. You are beautiful.

Here are some simpler phrases you may want to whisper to that special someone in your life:

Je t'aime.	I love you.
Je t'adore.	I adore you.
Tu me manques.	I miss you.
Je t'embrasse.	I kiss you.
Je rêve de toi.	I dream of you.
Tu es beau.	You are handsome.
Mon amour.	My love.
Mon chéri.	My dear.

"Hot" Meeting Spots

When I asked my Parisian girlfriend for advice on meeting men, she replied succinctly, "*Sors, sors, sors.*" Translation, "Go out, go out, go out." You will greatly increase your odds for meeting Mr. Right, or at least Mr. Intriguing, by spending most waking hours away from your hotel room. Every chance encounter has possibilities. The old adage, "You never know when you'll meet someone," has never been more applicable than in Paris, whether it be window-shopping on Rue du Faubourg-St.-Honoré or gazing at your favorite Picasso.

You can and will meet men all over Paris, but certain places and activities are more conducive than others. Anywhere there is a concentration of men is a good bet—men's stores, restaurants in the business district, nightclubs, sporting events, you name it.

HOT RESTAURANTS & CAFES

Here is a well-kept secret shared by my Parisian girlfriends. During lunch time, restaurants located near the main business centers are full of male patrons, and not many women! My friends go to these restaurants specifically to meet men, and you can too. Two neighborhoods to investigate are Place Vendôme (1st *arrondissement*) and the Champs-Elysées area (8th *arrondissement*). When exploring on your own, look for places bustling with activity and tables packed closely together. Noontime is usually too early, so plan to go around 1:00 P.M.

A girlfriend and I had a storybook lunch on Avenue Montaigne near the Champs-Elysées at Bar des Théâtres. No sooner did we sit down than the waiter brought complimentary glasses of wine offered by a tanned, blond Frenchman seated two tables away. We thanked him through our blushes, and after some minutes of glancing back and forth, the French woman seated between us offered to exchange places with him. Who says the French aren't friendly?

Our admirer, Chistopher, was a French actor working on a television soap opera for the BBC. He invited us to dinner that same evening and taught my girlfriend how to eat raw oysters.

I've had the most success meeting Frenchmen in cafés, restaurants, and nightclubs. These are settings where everyone is relaxed and in the mood to socialize. Plus, you have a captive audience, which gives you time to observe candidates and start to form an opinion about their desirability. Sounds calculated? It is!

Round-the-Clock Meeting Places

Here are the cafés and restaurants that are *plus populaire* (most popular) at all times of the day and night. Many of these places have bars, which, of course, are the best places to initiate a conversation. In particular, the bars at Bar des Théâtres, Mexico Café, and Le Telegraphe tend to be hopping in the early evening. If you prefer to meet fellow Americans, there is a list of American Watering Holes on page 63. Romantic restaurants in which to cozy up with your loved one are listed in Chapter Six.

BAR DES THEATRES ♥

As you enter, the tiny bar always seems to be packed and lively. This spot is popular with theatergoers looking for a light meal.

6 Avenue Montaigne
Phone: 47–23–34–63
8th *arrondissement*
Métro: Alma-Marceau

BRASSERIE STELLA

This unpretentious brasserie is the local eatery for the chic *seizième* (16th) crowd.

133 Avenue Victor-
  Hugo
Phone: 47–27–60–54
16th *arrondissement*
Métro: Victor-Hugo

CARETTE

Located in Place du Trocadéro, this is a popular hangout for the preppie inhabitants of the area. Carette is best known for its desserts and afternoon tea.

4 Place du Trocadéro
Phone: 47–27–88–56
16th *arrondissement*
Métro: Trocadéro

CHORUS CAFE

Adjoining the Bourse, or French Stock Exchange, this is a great neighborhood for meeting what Parisian women call "the golden boys" who work there.

23 Rue St.-Marc
Phone: 42–96–81–00
2nd *arrondissement*
Métro: Bourse

DEUX MAGOTS

The quintessential Parisian café, Deux Magots has been popular for decades among the literati. In warm weather, street performers put on a show on the sidewalk.

6 Place St.-Germain-
  des-Prés
Phone: 45–48–55–25
6th *arrondissement*
Métro: St.-Germain-
  des-Prés

Deux Magots.

FOUQUET'S

Smack in the middle of the Champs-Elysées, Fouquet's still manages to lure the *crème de Paris*. Behind the bar is a sign in French that translates to, "Single women are not admitted at the bar." I was told that this applies only to the bar itself, not to the adjoining tables.

99 Avenue des
 Champs-Elysées
Phone: 47–23–70–60
8th *arrondissement*
Métro: George-V

MEXICO CAFE

Owner Jean-Pierre Jabouille has the reputation for being quite a *bon vivant*, which isn't surprising since he used to be one of the top race car drivers in France.

1 Place de Mexico
Phone: 47–27–96–98
16th *arrondissement*
Métro: Trocadéro

LE TELEGRAPHE

Princess Stephanie of Monaco held her engagement party here—and the wedding was called off a month later. There is a large bar for socializing and stylish Art Déco furnishings. The crowd is *très chic*.

41 Rue de Lille
Phone: 40–15–06–65
7th *arrondissement*
Métro: Solférino

American Watering Holes

If you're in the mood to make the acquaintance of fellow Americans, here are a few good places to start. American restaurants are also becoming a big hit with Parisians, so the three listed below are likely to have French clients as well as compatriots.

AMERICAN CHURCH

This church is a focal point for the activities of Americans living in or just visiting Paris. The church posts social activities on the bulletin board, publishes a monthly newsletter, etc.

65 Quai d'Orsay
Phone: 47–05–07–99
7th *arrondissement*
Métro: Invalides or
  Alma-Marceau

AMERICAN EXPRESS OFFICE

Most American visitors to Paris pass through here to exchange traveler's checks for francs, to pick up a message, to buy a ticket for a concert—or just to hear English spoken and be around Yanks for a brief time.

11 Rue Scribe
Phone: 47–77–77–07
9th *arrondissement*
Métro: Opéra

CITY ROCK CAFE

This is part of the Hard Rock Café chain popularized in the States, with the trademark Cadillac and photos of film stars. It serves hamburgers, salads, brownies, and other American standards.

13 Rue de Berri
Phone: 43–59–52–09
8th *arrondissement*
Métro: George-V
Cards: AE, MC, V

HARRY'S BAR

Opened in 1911, Harry's Bar has always been a watering hole for American expatriates, including F. Scott Fitzgerald and Ernest Hemingway. In fact, George Gershwin is said to have conceived of "An American in Paris" here. Live piano music is provided from 10:00 P.M. to 2:00 A.M. Hot dogs are served all the time.

5 Rue Daunou
Phone: 42–61–71–14
2nd *arrondissement*
Métro: Opéra
Cards: AE

JOE ALLEN

This is the place to get solid American fare— spareribs, chile con carne, apple pie. It's part of a chain started in Los Angeles and New York.

30 Rue Pierre-Lescot
Phone: 42–36–70–13
1st *arrondissement*
Métro: Etienne-
  Marcel
Cards: MC, V

The French View of
Extramarital Diversions

The French attitude towards promiscuity and adultery has long been one of acceptance and accommodation. Consequently, you should be aware that some married Frenchmen are always on the lookout for a quick liaison. The following excerpts from Letitia Jett-Guichard's article "The Thoroughly Modern Mistress" vividly illustrate the French ethic.

"President François Mitterrand, commenting on the Anglo-Saxon preoccupation with extramarital diversions, put the subject in perspective. 'If I had to choose my ministers on the basis of marital fidelity,' he told the press, 'I would be unable to put together a government. . . . '"

* * *

"When the subject happens to arise, as it often does at the choicest soirées as a respite from endless discourses on food and politics, it is assumed as a matter of course that men have mistresses, and morality is not at issue. . . ."

* * *

"The American horror of adultery, powerful enough to end the career of a presidential hopeful, is hard to comprehend for the French. 'What you Americans forget—and it's not your fault,' says a young woman doctor, recently married, 'is that there is infidelity and there is infidelity. Even in my generation, the family comes first, that sense of continuity, not some obsession with the sexual fidelity of your husband or wife. I love my husband and he loves me, but we are realists. If he has a *petite amie*, I don't want to know about it, and if I take a lover, I won't tell him.'"

Excerpts from "The Thoroughly Modern Mistress" by Letitia Jett-Guichard, in *Avenue*, January 1989. Reprinted with permission.

Best Bets at Lunch Time

The following restaurants abound with businessmen during lunch time.

LE BOEUF SUR LE TOIT

The crowd here is very elegant and smart, with lots of dapper businessmen from the adjoining *bureaux* (offices).

34 Rue du Colisée
Phone: 43–59–83–80
8th *arrondissement*
Métro: Franklin-D.-
Roosevelt

CHEZ ANDRE ♥

The tables are placed side by side, so it's very easy to strike up a conversation with people seated nearby. The mood is informal and lively.

12 Rue Marbeuf
Phone: 47–20–59–57
8th *arrondissement*
Métro: Franklin-D.-
Roosevelt

CHEZ EDGARD

Many politicians and journalists who work in the area come here for their *déjeuner*, lunch. You might be wise to refer to The French View of Extramarital Diversions on page 64, since a lot of these men are married.

4 Rue Marbeuf
Phone: 47–20–51–15
8th *arrondissement*
Métro: Franklin-D.-
Roosevelt

LE VAUDEVILLE

The ratio here is about nine men to every woman. Again, the tables are very close, so you can easily get to know your neighbor. But, as the following story demonstrates, it's more difficult to talk to the guy across the room.

29 Rue Vivienne
Phone: 42–33–39–31
2nd *arrondissement*
Métro: Bourse

To get things started, establishing eye contact is always the first step, but, as you'll see from the following example, generating a conversation is often a bit more difficult.

While researching this book, I went to Le Vaudeville, a busy restaurant across from the French Bourse (stock exchange), for lunch with an attractive American girlfriend living in Paris. She was rather skeptical about the whole outing, but I explained that, "I have to do this for my readers, and besides I hear the place is teeming with attractive men." Well, no sooner did we sit down than my girlfriend spotted a very good-looking Frenchman (literally tall, dark, and handsome) seated by himself a few tables away. Their eye contact began flitting back and forth, fast and furious. Interest was definitely established on both sides.

We needed a plan, a way to start a conversation with this dreamboat. So we beckoned to the maître d' and explained that I was writing a guide and would like to speak with one or two of the customers, possibly the man sitting by himself a few tables away. The maître d' replied that he couldn't possibly trouble such a prestigious and regular customer, and then offered to introduce us to an elderly couple that was just finishing their meal. Needless to say, we struck out on this one. But we did learn that Mr. Handsome goes there frequently. I think my girlfriend will be going back.

HOT DISCOS

Discos, known as *boîtes de nuit* (night boxes), are exciting meeting places. If you're looking for a count or prince, the exclusive discos are one of your best bets. Parisians love to party late, so most discos don't open until midnight. It is very common for people to dance by themselves, and don't be surprised if you get approached on the dance floor.

Following are the most popular discos in Paris. The métro stops aren't listed, because you should catch a cab at that late hour.

LES BAINS

Similar to New York's infamous Studio 54 of days gone by, Les Bains, when crowded, will let you in only if you have a hip "look." Just play up the fact that you're a visiting American; that should do the trick.

7 Rue du Bourg-l'Abbé
Phone: 48–87–01–80
3rd *arrondissement*
Cards: None
Admission: 120 francs
  ($25)
Open: 12 A.M.–5 A.M.

LE BUS PALLADIUM

Loud and lively, Le Bus Palladium is popular with the younger set.

6 Rue Fontaine
Phone: 48–74–54–99
9th *arrondissement*
Cards: Not accepted for admission, but all accepted inside
Admission: 110 francs ($22)
Open: 11:30 P.M.–4:00 A.M.

CASTEL-PRINCESSE ♥

This is a very private club run by Jean Castel so that his friends can party away the night hours. It's best to ask a French friend to take you.

15 Rue Princesse
Phone: 43–26–90–22
6th *arrondissement*
Cards: AE, MC, V
Open: 9:30 P.M.

PALACE

The Palace is big and loud and caters to the younger set. The DJs are from England.

8 Rue du Faubourg-Montmartre
Phone: 42–46–10–87
9th *arrondissement*
Cards: AE, MC, V
Admission: 130 francs ($26)
Open: 11:00 P.M.–6:00 A.M.

REGINE'S

Régine has become world-renowned for her clubs in many major cities. Here, again, the club is private, but my girlfriends and I have managed to get in. One way is to ask your hotel concierge to reserve a table in the adjoining restaurant for dinner, and then stay afterwards to enjoy the disco.

49 Rue de Ponthieu
Phone: 43–59–21–60
8th *arrondissement*
Cards: AE, MC, V

How to Strike Up a Conversation

Most of us experience "shy attacks" and have some difficulty in initiating an encounter. There are two key steps to striking up a conversation with the Frenchman who catches your fancy. The first step is to capture his eye by looking your best. The second step is to show an open, engaging manner. Many Frenchmen have told me about women they approached and did not pursue because of the woman's cool response. If you are interested, establishing eye contact and smiling are the best ways to let the dashing Frenchman at the next table know you are receptive. In addition, here are a few ploys you can use in a pinch:

- Carry a guidebook—an obvious indication that you're an exotic foreigner.
- Ask for advice or help in taking a photo.
- Hold a map and appear to be lost.
- If you are with a group of people and don't want to make a move in front of them, when you depart, leave something behind that you will have to go back and fetch a few minutes later. Sunglasses or an umbrella serve dual purposes here.
- Wear a fun or eccentric piece of clothing that invites comment.
- Be creative and make things happen.

BEST PICK-UP LINE
I went to a popular restaurant, whose name will go unmentioned, with a Frenchman who was showing me the town. When he stepped away from our table for a few minutes, I started petting a dog who was with two guys at an adjoining table. One of the guys turned to me and said (in French), "Our dog would like your phone number."

For example, daring but true, on my first trip to Paris my girlfriend and I decided to follow the custom established by young guitar players who perform in front of cafés for a few francs. One evening, we dressed to kill, caught a taxi to the Champs-Elysées, and proceeded to sing two songs in front of Fouquet's. "What two songs?" you ask. Would you believe, "Diamonds Are a Girl's Best Friend" and "I've Been Working on the Railroad," the only two songs whose lyrics I could remember? Needless to say, we brought the house down, and one charming man observed, "Girls, I've been coming here for twenty years and haven't seen anything like this." I'm sure he hadn't. He then whisked us off to Régine's, where we celebrated with champagne and danced the night away.

Be Selective and Take Precautions

As you are putting your most vivacious foot forward, evaluate the situation and the man, and be selective. There is no harm in talking with someone for a few minutes to gauge his sincerity, his motives, and his appeal. But there is also no need to invest hours of your precious time with someone you realize is not for you. Here are some of the criteria I use:

- Does he have manners?
- Does he speak English?
- Is he educated and cultured?
- What are his interests?
- Am I attracted to this man?
- What are my expectations?

A few times, I've found myself in dangerous situations when girlfriends brought along French guys who were rude and aggressive. As in any culture, you will encounter a range of personalities. Protect yourself by keeping your first few meetings in public settings and by using public transportation rather than getting into a stranger's car.

In France, as elsewhere, there is a difference between being friendly and giving a man the impression that you're trying to pick him up. Obviously, the latter is not a safe or advisable tack to take. Most Frenchmen are respectful, especially if you make it very clear in the beginning that you want to start by being "just friends."

Most Frenchmen enjoy *la chasse* (the chase) as much as, if not more than, *la conquête* (the conquest). If your new beau is pushing too hard, too soon for intimate involvement, you should bail out. My experience has been that the Frenchman worth having is the one who waits for a cue from you before beginning the seduction.

If the going does get serious, you should insist on using protection. In this day and age, there is no alternative. The risks far outweigh any inconvenience.

Romantic Rendezvous

You won't need to look far to find romantic ways and places to spend time with your loved one or with that dashing Frenchman you just met. We all have our favorite rendezvous. For some, it is strolling the side streets on the island of Ile Saint-Louis while eating ice cream from Berthillon. For others, it is a candlelit dinner for two at the Jules Verne restaurant atop the Eiffel Tower, with a breathtaking view of the city. For still others, it is staying at l'Hôtel, where no two rooms are alike and celebrities and honeymooners reside incognito.

For me, it is spending the afternoon exploring a museum or new exhibit together, and then enjoying a *tête-à-tête* at Angelina's *salon de thé*. Later, the evening begins with a glass of champagne at one of the bars in the Ritz Hotel before going to Michel Rostang's restaurant for a five-course nouvelle cuisine delight. I love to top off the evening by kicking up my heels at one of the discos.

The simple, spontaneous pleasures are just as romantic and memorable—strolling through a park, sipping a *café crème* in a sidewalk café, or window-shopping on one of the elegant boulevards. No matter what the pastime, *Paris will embrace you!*

One last piece of advice. Don't set high expectations for lasting relationships. Some women have made wonderful friendships, but this is not the general rule. The Latin tendency is to live and love without inhibition—and without plans for the future. Enjoy the moment and your fond memories.

The rest of this book gives you plenty of ideas for ways to share time with your loved one while enjoying the magic and wonder that is Paris.

Romance in Paris is an unforgettable experience!

5. La Culture

Learn About History and Art Firsthand

Learning about Parisian culture is a wonderfully participatory experience. All you need to do is step outside your hotel and start walking. The *centre de la ville* (center of the city) is a special world unto itself with new discoveries at every turn.

You will come across many monuments that seem like old friends because you've seen them so many times before in movies, on television, and in photos—the Tour Eiffel piercing the sky; Place de la Concorde, with its fountains illuminated at night; and the Arc de Triomphe standing watch over the Champs-Elysées. No, you're not in a dream. This is the real thing!

I subscribe to the school of serendipity, exploring without a set timetable and allowing the city to unveil herself at my feet. The French Tourist Office (see page 31) can recommend walking routes that include important sights and points of interest, and the Suggested Reading List (see page 173) offers other sources to enhance your knowledge of *la culture française*. This chapter highlights the key historical sights, museums, bookstores, and concert and exhibition halls. Historical sights found on the periphery of Paris and in the surrounding countryside—Versailles and Giverny, for instance—are discussed in Chapter Ten. My favorite choices are indicated with a heart ♥ rating.

"Paris is the antithesis of those ancient cities in which the sanctified monuments are separated from one another by street after street in which no one could wish to linger, let alone to live. Paris is in itself a work of art—and greater, in this respect, than any of its individual buildings."
—*John Russell*
Paris

71

HISTORICAL SIGHTS

Paris is steeped in a fascinating history, and many monuments have been constructed to celebrate past glories. Over the centuries, each ruler has left his mark by commissioning the leading architect of that time to design yet another palace or square or garden, and that tradition continues today.

The following are a handful of Paris' most famous landmarks. You will see many other monuments and statues during your trip, since they're on almost every corner. Parisians are very proud of their achievements.

One of the best ways to catch a glimpse of the major historical sights in a brief period of time is to take a half-day bus tour of the city (see page 34). Another way to see many of the important structures from a scenic vantage point is to take one of the boat rides along the Seine (details on page 140). Both are available by day and night.

L'ARC DE TRIOMPHE

8th *arrondissement*
Métro: Charles-de-Gaulle-Etoile

Standing majestically at the foot of the Champs-Elysées, the Arc de Triomphe was commissioned by Napoleon in 1806 to commemorate his victories. It now houses the tomb of France's unknown soldier and is at the center of the busiest traffic hub in Paris—the Place de l'Etoile (*étoile* means star), now known as Place Charles-de-Gaulle, from which twelve avenues radiate. From the observation deck, you have an excellent view of the Eiffel Tower, the Champs-Elysées, and the Louvre beyond.

NOTRE DAME

4th *arrondissement*
Métro: Cité, Hôtel-de-Ville, Maubert-Mutualité, or St.-Michel

One of the great Gothic cathedrals of Europe, Notre Dame is located on the Ile de la Cité, one of two small islands in the Seine. Its construction began in 1163 and took almost a century to complete. The size of Notre Dame is overpowering. From the transept you can see the Seine, both islands, and the connecting bridges. The surrounding neighborhood has wonderful examples of Renaissance architecture, and is one of the most expensive districts in Paris. The Conciergerie and Sainte-Chapelle are within walking distance.

Notre Dame.

PLACE DE LA CONCORDE

8th *arrondissement*
Métro: Concorde

Located on the eastern end of the Champs-Elysées, Place de la Concorde is a busy thoroughfare adjacent to the Tuileries Gardens. Complete with mermaids and sea nymphs in fountains and a 3,300-year-old Egyptian obelisk, it is especially lovely when floodlit at night (reminiscent of a suspenseful movie chase scene, and many have been shot here). To add to the intrigue, just remind yourself that this was the scene of the Reign of Terror during the French Revolution. Thousands of people died here under the blade of the guillotine, including King Louis XVI and his Queen, Marie Antoinette.

PLACE VENDOME

1st *arrondissement*
Métro: Tuileries or
  Concorde

This is the site of the luxurious Ritz Hotel, and one of the choicest locales in Paris. The square was designed for Louis XIV by Mansart at the end of the seventeenth century and is considered a great architectural achievement. Most of the buildings house prestigious businesses, and there are a few very elegant shops, including Cartier and Van Cleef et Arpels.

The Eiffel Tower.

LA TOUR EIFFEL

The Eiffel Tower celebrated its one hundredth anniversary in May 1989. What is now a Paris landmark was very controversial during its construction. Labeled "useless and monstrous" at the time, it was the tallest structure in the world, and was scheduled to be torn down after twenty years. Thankfully, it has endured and has become a symbol of Paris. If you're feeling ambitious, you can climb the 1,655 steps to the top instead of taking the elevator. In addition to the viewing platforms, the Jules Verne restaurant in the tower offers a spectacular view and is very romantic at night.

7th *arrondissement*
Métro: Champ de
  Mars-Tour Eiffel

MUSEUMS

There are so many different enchanting museums in Paris that whole books have been devoted to the subject. This section describes many of the well-known museums and some of the more intimate museums devoted to French artists and French history.

The smaller, less crowded museums are my preference. Musée Rodin is surrounded by beautiful gardens, with Rodin's sculpture interspersed throughout. Musée Marmottan is a charming two-story townhouse with a cache of works by Claude Monet. And Musée Carnavalet depicts the history of Paris in winding, interconnected rooms with squeaky wooden floors and an eclectic mixture of objects; we're talking old.

The admission costs range from about $4 to $6, and museums are generally closed on Mondays.

CENTRE GEORGES POMPIDOU

This is not a must-see, but deserves mention—if only because of the ongoing debate over its architecture. The French love to argue over architecture. This five-story mixture of steel and glass exposes the building's brightly color-coded heating ducts, ventilation shafts, and stairways. The center houses a modern art museum, public library, film archive, and cinema; it is also referred to as the Beaubourg.

19 Rue Beaubourg
Phone: 42–77–12–33
4th *arrondissement*
Métro: Rambuteau,
  Hôtel-de-Ville, or
  Châtelet

L'ORANGERIE

Located opposite the Louvre at the west end of the Tuileries Gardens, this former citrus nursery displays works by Renoir, Monet, Cézanne, Picasso, and Matisse. Highlights include Claude Monet's eight giant water lily murals on the lower floor.

Off Place de la
  Concorde
Phone: 42–97–48–16
1st *arrondissement*
Métro: Concorde

Place des Vosges.

MUSEE CARNAVALET

The Carnavalet's stated purpose is to illustrate the history of Paris, from its most distant origins to the present day. Formerly the famous hotel of the Marquise de Sévigné, it is now owned by the City of Paris. This 400-year-old mansion is crammed with furniture, paintings, clothes, and *objets d'art*. The section devoted to the French Revolution offers one of the most complete and provocative documentations of this difficult period, including furnishings used by the royal family during its imprisonment and several small-scale models of the deadly guillotine. While you are in the Marais district, it will be well worth your while to stroll a few blocks to Place des Vosges, the oldest square in Paris and one of the most beautiful. Created for Henri IV in 1605, it was at one time the major dueling ground of Europe.

23 Rue de Sévigné
Phone: 42-72-21-13
3rd *arrondissement*
Métro: St.-Paul

MUSEE DE CLUNY

Many people consider the Cluny the most attractive museum in Paris. One of the few medieval buildings still in existence, it is devoted mainly to the French art and crafts of the Middle Ages. In the garden are ruins of Roman baths.

6 Place Paul-Painlevé
Phone: 43–25–62–00
5th *arrondissement*
Métro: St.-Michel or
   Odéon

MUSEE D'ORSAY

Musée d'Orsay is a recently converted railroad station. Designed by a woman, Gae Aulenti, the museum houses art created from 1848 to 1914 on three levels, with sculpture scattered throughout and sunlight streaming in through the translucent roof. The large collection of impressionist works was formerly displayed in the Musée Jeu de Paume.

The museum's roof-top café is for casual snacks and has an outdoor terrace overlooking the Seine and Notre Dame. The more formal restaurant on the middle level is a lovely place to break for lunch and a far cry from most museum cafeterias. This is a fun museum experience.

1 Rue de Bellechasse
Phone: 40–49–48–14
7th *arrondissement*
Métro: Solférino

Musée d'Orsay. ▶

MUSEE MARMOTTAN   ♥

2 Rue Louis-Boilly
Phone: 42–24–07–02
16th *arrondissement*
Métro: La Muette

My favorite! Tucked away in a nineteenth century townhouse adjacent to a park in the 16th *arrondissement*, Musée Marmottan houses the largest single collection of Claude Monet's work. Over sixty-five original paintings, pastels, and drawings are displayed, alongside a sampling of Monet's notebooks and palettes. One of Monet's signature works, *Impression, Soleil Levant (Impression, Sunrise)*—from which the name "impressionist" was derived for that whole period and style of painting—was stolen in broad daylight by masked robbers during visiting hours a few years ago. Fortunately, it was recently recovered by French police and is back on display. Marmottan is one of the most rewarding museum experiences in Paris, and one of the least crowded.

MUSEE NATIONAL DU LOUVRE

Phone: 42–60–39–26
1st *arrondissement*
Métro: Louvre or
  Palais-Royal

The Louvre is the largest building in Paris and the most well-known museum in Europe. Recently, it has received a great deal of publicity for the new glass pyramid structures in the courtyard. Designed by I.M. Pei, these structures, which protect the front of the time-worn edifice, are a good example of France's emphasis on preserving its national monuments. The new entrance, through the larger pyramid in the middle, is one of the most modern and well-organized in the world. It is so streamlined that you can buy your admission ticket from a vending machine.

The Louvre possesses over 400,000 works of art, and the sheer size and grandeur are a bit intimidating, as are the crowds. I don't normally recommend guided tours, but in this instance it will give you the opportunity to see the highlights, learn about the building's fascinating history, and avoid getting lost in the maze of 224 halls. And you won't accidentally miss seeing the Mona Lisa.

The Louvre Pyramids.

The gift shop is well stocked with art books and smaller items that make great presents for friends back home.

MUSEE PICASSO

This opulent seventeenth century mansion in the Marais, a charming neighborhood near the Bastille, holds the largest collection of Picasso's work. When Picasso died in 1973, leaving no will, his heirs donated part of his personal collection to France in lieu of the $65 million in inheritance taxes. Musée Picasso, the beneficiary of this donation, opened a few years ago.

5 Rue de Thorigny
Phone: 42–71–25–21
3rd *arrondissement*
Métro: St.-Paul or
   St.-Sébastien-Froissart

MUSEE RODIN ♥

77 Rue de Varenne
Phone: 47–05–01–34
7th *arrondissement*
Métro: Varenne

This is a must-see. Surrounded by one of the largest gardens in Paris, the museum provides an idyllic setting for many of Auguste Rodin's beautiful sculptures. The building itself was once home and studio to many artists, including Henri Matisse, Isadora Duncan, and, of course, Rodin. The room containing Rodin's *The Sculptor With His Muse* also displays several works by Camille Claudel, the talented sculptress who at seventeen became Rodin's muse, model, and lover.

Rodin said, "Intelligence designs, but the heart does the modeling." *Le Penseur (The Thinker)*, his best-known work, stands in the garden over his tomb.

BOOKSTORES

Bookstores in Paris have an ambience and history all their own. Ernest Hemingway, Gertrude Stein, F. Scott Fitzgerald, and many other American writers congregated in Paris in the 1920s and contributed to the artistic renaissance of that era. In *A Moveable Feast*, Hemingway wrote fondly about his time spent at Shakespeare & Company, a popular bookstore still in existence, "On a cold windswept street, this was a warm, cheerful place with a big stove in winter, tables and shelves of books, new books in the window, and photographs on the wall of famous writers dead and living."

The following have good selections of books in English. They are closed on Sundays.

BRENTANO'S
37 Avenue de l'Opéra
Phone: 42–61–52–50
2nd *arrondissement*
Métro: Opéra or Pyramides

GALIGNANI
224 Rue de Rivoli
Phone: 42–60–76–07
1st *arrondissement*
Métro: Concorde

VILLAGE VOICE
6 Rue Princesse
Phone: 46–33–36–47
6th *arrondissement*
Métro: Mabillon

W.H. SMITH & SON
248 Rue de Rivoli
Phone: 42–60–37–97
1st *arrondissement*
Métro: Concorde

SHAKESPEARE & COMPANY
37 Rue de la Bûcherie
Phone: None
5th *arrondissement*
Métro: Maubert-Mutualité

CONCERTS AND EXHIBITIONS

One of the best ways to enjoy French culture and to mingle with the *vrai français* (real French) is to attend a concert or exhibition. Don't be put off by the language barrier. You can attend a concert, ballet, opera, special exhibit, or even a musical comedy, and gain much from the experience.

The American Express Office and Paris Tourism Office have counters set up to help you make reservations. There is also a phone recording in English for cultural information: 47–20–88–98. Your hotel concierge is another resource.

For you daring, independent types, there are a few French publications listing upcoming events that can be purchased at most newsstands (called *kiosks*); *Pariscope, L'Officiel,* and *7 à Paris* are put out weekly. *Passion,* a guide to Paris written in English, is published every few months and is available at many international newsstands in the United States and at the *kiosks* in Paris.

A few concert and exhibition venues stand out for their beauty and character.

COMEDIE FRANCAISE

Built by King Louis XIV in the late 1600s, this enchanting theater has lively performances in French.

2 Rue de Richelieu
Phone: 40–15–00–15
1st *arrondissement*
Métro: Palais-Royal

GRAND PALAIS

Adjacent to Place de la Concorde, the Grand Palais hosts revolving exhibitions.

Avenue Winston
 Churchill
8th *arrondissement*
Métro: Champs-
 Elysées-Clémenceau

LOUVRE

Many concerts are held in this charming setting in the heart of the city.

Place du Carrousel
Phone: 40–20–52–29
1st *arrondissement*
Métro: Louvre

OPERA

Now that a new opera house has been built at the Bastille, this, the original opera house, specializes in ballet performances.

8 Rue Scribe
Phone: 47–42–57–50
9th *arrondissement*
Métro: Opéra

The Original Opéra House.

SAINTE-CHAPELLE

Located on Ile de la Cité near Notre Dame, this church boasts immense stained-glass windows that are considered the finest in Paris. Many concerts are held here.

4 Boulevard du Palais
Phone: 43–54–30–09
4th *arrondissement*
Métro: Cité

THEATRE DU CHATELET

This large 2,100-seat theater offers opera, ballet, symphonies, and recitals.

2 Rue Edouard-
Colonne
Phone: 40–28–28–28
1st *arrondissement*
Métro: Châtelet

Even if you're normally not a museum buff or theatergoer, the sights and sounds of Paris are bound to entrance you. The French culture is palpable—visible on every street, in every statue, fountain, and ancient building—and is evolving all the time. The thrill of seeing the Eiffel Tower, Place de la Concorde, and other awe-inspiring monuments will last a lifetime. And, if you're like me, Paris will draw you back time and time again.

6. La Cuisine

Delight in French Taste Treats

Parisian restaurants and cafés offer a delicious glimpse into the French way of life. The French have had a love affair with their cuisine for centuries. Dining is an integral part of each day, and meals can last for hours. Choices range from neighborhood mom-and-pop bistros to three-star gourmet restaurants.

If you want to grab a snack or prepare a picnic, the variety and abundance of mouth-watering food shops are very tempting—the *pâtisserie* and *boulangerie* for fresh-baked goods and flaky croissants; the fresh produce *marché* (market); the *fromagerie* with hundreds of varieties of cheeses; the *boucherie* for meat; and the *charcuterie* for beautifully prepared *pâtés*, salads, meats, and quiches, all ready to eat.

This chapter highlights some of the most popular and traditional French dining spots, romantic restaurants, wine bars, gourmet specialty stores, and cooking classes. You'll also learn about open-air markets where you can find delicious snacks for an inexpensive picnic lunch. *Bon appétit!*

CAFES

Cafés offer a perfect setting to while away a few hours sipping a *café au lait* or *coupe de champagne*. In *The Food Lover's Guide to Paris*, Patricia Wells writes, "As diverse as Parisians themselves, the cafés serve as an extension of the French living room, a place to start and end the day, to gossip and debate, a place for seeing and being seen."

Cafés started at the end of the seventeenth century as all-male establishments. Eventually, women were allowed in specially designated rooms, but they were still prohibited from sitting alone on the terraces until well into this century. In the 1920s, American writers were drawn to Paris, and they frequented many now-famous cafés on the Left Bank.

The following cafés are the most well known, *bien connu*, and popular. They all serve meals and are open late. The average cost for a *café au lait* is 22 francs, or a little over $4. (Café terms are listed on page 85.)

CAFE DE FLORE

Sartre, Simone de Beauvoir, and Camus used to gather here to discuss the ideas that led to existentialism. The literati still frequent Flore in the late afternoon.

172 Boulevard St.-
 Germain
Phone: 45–48–55–26
6th *arrondissement*
Métro: St. Germain-
 des-Prés
Cards: AE

CAFE DE LA PAIX

This is the nicest café near the Opéra, American Embassy, and Galeries Lafayette. The sidewalk facing the Opéra seems less touristy—meaning this is where the Parisians sit.

12 Boulevard des
 Capucines
Phone: 42–68–12–13
9th *arrondissement*
Métro: Opéra
Cards: AE, MC, V

LA CLOSERIE DES LILAS

Once a lilac-shaded country tavern, Closerie des Lilas was Hemingway's watering hole and his favorite spot to converse with fellow writers. Today's high prices don't draw many struggling artists, but this café is very fashionable and smart—and good for people-watching.

171 Boulevard
 Montparnasse
Phone: 43–26–70–50
6th *arrondissement*
Métro: Port-Royal
Cards: AE, MC, V

Café Terms

For most of us, one of the first places we go after arriving in Paris is a lively neighborhood café—to relax, to soak up the atmosphere, and to tune in to Paris' special rhythm. A major hurdle to your adjustment will be the difference in language. Here are translations of some basic café terms. Other food terms are listed on pages 94–95.

Café noir (or espresso)	Plain, very strong black coffee
Café au lait (or *café crème*)	Coffee with steamed milk
Décaféiné or *décaf*	Decaffeinated coffee
Café filtre	Uses drip method, less strong
Infusion	Herb tea
Thé au lait	Tea with milk
Thé au citron	Tea with lemon
Thé nature	Plain tea
Chocolat chaud	Hot chocolate

LA COUPOLE

La Coupole is a longstanding Paris institution. I'm told that well-to-do older French women used to come here in the afternoons to meet good-looking young men who would be willing to serve as companions for a short time. After the new owners rebuilt La Coupole in 1988, many felt that it had lost its former luster, but it is still very crowded.

102 Boulevard Montparnasse
Phone: 43–20–14–20
14th *arrondissement*
Métro: Vavin
Cards: AE, MC, V

How Many Courses in a French Meal?

A formal French meal is a ceremony developed to an art form that lasts an entire evening. While a typical American dinner consists of three or four courses, a French *dîner* can include as many as ten courses. We're talking staying power and pacing yourself—particularly if you love desserts, as I do. Thankfully, the portions are small. Here is the normal sequence of courses.

1. Apéritif (cocktail before meal)
2. Soup
3. Fish dish
4. Meat dish
5. Salad
6. Cheese plate
7. Dessert or fruit
8. Coffee
9. After-dinner drink, such as cognac

LES DEUX MAGOTS

Deux Magots faces Paris' oldest church, Saint-Germain-des-Prés, built in the sixth century. Deux Magots is newer (1875) and is the most inviting and popular of the cafés on the Left Bank. And it's open every day of the year, from early morning until well past midnight.

6 Place St.-Germain
Phone: 45–48–55–25
6th *arrondissement*
Métro: St.-Germain-des-Prés
Cards: None

FOUQUET'S

Fouquet's is more elegant and formal than the other cafés and draws a very international crowd. Even though I generally recommend staying away from the Champs-Elysées, this is worth the detour.

99 Avenue des Champs-Elysées
Phone: 47–23–70–60
8th *arrondissement*
Métro: George-V
Cards: AE, MC, V

LIPP

The Lipp brasserie opened a few years after Café de Flore, and specializes in German dishes and large mugs of beer. The National Assembly is nearby, and many politicians, including President Mitterrand, stop here for a late snack. Try to get seated on the ground floor where all the action is.

151 Boulevard St.-Germain
Phone: 45–48–53–91
6th *arrondissement*
Métro: St.-Germain-des-Prés
Cards: AE, MC, V

Restaurants

Many consider Paris to be the gastronomical capital of the world, and the French certainly hold this view. French chefs are viewed as national treasures and achieve the celebrity status reserved in most countries for actors and sports figures.

This section is broken into three categories: world-famous restaurants, up-and-coming restaurants, and my recommendations for other excellent restaurants by neighborhood. Restaurant customs are explained on page 88. Restaurants that are imbued with a romantic ambience are indicated with a heart ♥ rating.

WORLD-FAMOUS RESTAURANTS

A handful of the most famous restaurants, Jamin, Taillevent, Lucas-Carton, and La Tour d'Argent, are an experience unto themselves. The setting is formal—elegant and ornate; each individual plate takes hours to prepare and is presented as a work of art; and, of course, the prices are astronomical. The four restaurants just mentioned all run around 950 francs per person, without wine, which is around $200.

One way to cut down on the high cost is to order from the *prix fixe* (fixed price) menu, which offers a limited selection of dishes in a few courses. The *prix fixe* menu is offered more often at lunch than dinner and isn't available in all restaurants. It is also known as the *menu*.

JOEL ROBUCHON (JAMIN)

Chef Joël Robuchon is considered by French restaurant critics to be the best in the world, and has been at the top of the list for many years. He is noted for his tenacity in searching out the freshest ingredients. He then spends hours "capturing the true flavor."

32 Rue de Longchamp
Phone: 47–27–12–27
16th *arrondissement*
Métro: Trocadéro
Cards: AE, MC, V

LUCAS-CARTON

Located in a beautiful corner overlooking Place de la Madeleine, Lucas-Carton has Art Nouveau decor in a very formal setting. The service is impeccable. Alain Senderens is the chef and owner.

9 Place de la Madeleine
Phone: 42–65–22–90
8th *arrondissement*
Métro: Madeleine
Cards: MC, V

Restaurant Customs

Navigating French restaurant customs is an ongoing adventure. One never knows what to expect next. When in doubt, smile and preface your request with "*S'il vous plaît*," which means "If you please," and then forge ahead. Here are a few guidelines.

- It is always wise to phone ahead for reservations. Many restaurants are closed on weekends and in August. The top restaurants book a month or more ahead.
- In old-fashioned, formal restaurants, the prices are listed only on those menus handed to the men, or to just the host. Women can order to their hearts' content and be oblivious of the financial consequences.
- Some restaurants carry menus in English—usually the most expensive restaurants, as well as the cafés and bistros in the main tourist areas (Rue de Rivoli, the Champs-Elysées, and St.-Germain-des-Prés). For those times when an English menu is not provided, a glossary of French food terms can be found on pages 94–95.
- A good way to sample the chef's specialties is to order the *prix fixe* (fixed price) menu, which consists of three or four courses. Everything except drinks is included in one price. This is usually a better bargain than ordering *à la carte*, with each item being priced separately.
- Most of the time, a 15-percent tip is already included in the price. This is indicated by the term *service compris* (service included), found on the menu.
- In many restaurants, the light in the toilet doesn't go on until you lock the door. If there is a hostess in the bathroom, you should leave a few-franc tip.

TAILLEVENT

According to Patricia Wells, this is "Paris's most perfect restaurant." Owner Jean-Claude Vrinat, son of the founder, creates a harmonious balance of good food, warm service, and beautiful decor. The chef is Claude Deligne.

15 Rue Lammenais
Phone: 45–63–39–34
8th *arrondissement*
Métro: George-V
Cards: MC, V

LA TOUR D'ARGENT

This is possibly the best-known restaurant in Paris. Owner Claude Terrail is an institution, dapper and always sporting a blue "bachelor" flower in his lapel. Tables have a striking view of the Seine and Notre Dame. The house speciality is duck; however, the food here is not quite as good as that of the other three restaurants. Lunch is the best time to go for the *prix fixe* menu; dinner is more than twice as expensive.

15 Quai de la Tournelle
Phone: 43–54–23–31
5th *arrondissement*
Métro: Maubert-
  Mutualité
Cards: AE, MC, V

UP-AND-COMING RESTAURANTS

There are many wonderful restaurants that aren't quite as famous as those just listed, and so do not require reservations months in advance—although you will still need to book at least a few weeks ahead. Parisians pride themselves on discovering excellent restaurants with superb chefs that haven't yet achieved top status. Here is a compilation of the restaurants and chefs that will be among the most critically acclaimed in the decade to come.

These restaurants are all *très cher*, very expensive, so, when possible, the *prix fixe* amount is listed. Since these costs are subject to change, it's advisable to call ahead for the latest information.

L'AMBROISIE ♥

This is one of the most romantic restaurants in Paris. The chateau setting and forest tapestry wall hangings are complemented by huge vases of fresh-cut flowers. There are less than a dozen tables, so the atmosphere is *très intime*, very intimate. The food is superb, reflecting the three-star rating. And L'Ambroisie is in a charming location facing Place des Vosges, one of the prettiest squares in Paris.

9 Place des Vosges
Phone: 42–78–51–45
4th *arrondissement*
Métro: St.-Paul
Cards: MC, V

AMPHYCLES

This restaurant has been open for only a few years and is already receiving raves from critics in France and the United States. Chef-owner Philippe Groult is a disciple of Joël Robuchon of Jamin (see page 87), so it's no wonder the critics are making such a fuss. Amphycles is very popular with Parisians and seats only forty-five, so you need to reserve well ahead.

78 Avenue des Ternes
Phone: 40–68–01–01
17th *arrondissement*
Métro: Ternes or
  Pt.-Maillot
Cards: MC, V
Prix Fixe: 220 francs
  ($44), lunch

APICIUS

Chef Jean-Pierre Vigato specializes in classic French dishes. Madame Vigato, his wife, greets guests and presides over the dining room. The decor is modern and elegant.

122 Avenue de Villiers
Phone: 43–80–19–66
17th *arrondissement*
Métro: Péreire
Cards: AE, MC, V

CARRE DES FEUILLANTS

Chef Alain Dutournier specializes in his native southwest cuisine. His wife continues to run their first restaurant, Au Trou Gascon, an informal, less expensive, small restaurant. (Au Trou Gascon, Phone: 43–44–34–26.)

14 Rue de Castiglione
Phone: 42–86–82–82
1st *arrondissement*
Métro: Tuileries
Cards: AE, MC, V
Prix Fixe: 490 francs
  ($98), lunch and
  dinner

FAUGERON

This small gourmet restaurant is on a lovely street in the heart of the chic *seizième* (16th) *arrondissement*. Madame Faugeron runs the dining room and is acclaimed for her *bon accueil* (warm welcome). The wine steward, Jean-Claude Jambon, won the 1986 award for best sommelier.

52 Rue de Longchamp
Phone: 47–04–24–53
16th *arrondissement*
Métro: Trocadéro
Cards: MC, V
Prix Fixe: 310 francs
  ($62), lunch

GUY SAVOY

Savoy gets very high ratings from French restaurant critics for his gourmet food. The desserts are divine!

18 Rue Troyon
Phone: 43–80–40–61
17th *arrondissement*
Métro: Charles-de-
  Gaulle-Etoile
Cards: AE, MC, V

MICHEL ROSTANG

Chef Rostang is a rising star on the Paris scene. He was the first of the top chefs to open an adjoining bistro to offer customers a more casual, simple dining experience at half the cost. His Bistro d'à Côté has a fun, rustic decor, and the food is excellent. (Bistro d'à Côté, Phone: 42–67–05–81.)

20 Rue Rennequin
Phone: 47–63–40–77
17th *arrondissement*
Métro: Ternes
Cards: AE, MC, V
Prix Fixe: 250 francs
($50), lunch

QUINZE AVENUE MONTAIGNE

Known as La Maison Blanche before moving to this upscale address, Quinze Avenue Montaigne has delicious food and an elegant clientele. And, of course, the prices are very high.

15 Avenue Montaigne
Phone: 47–23–55–99
8th *arrondissement*
Métro: Alma-Marceau
Cards: MC, V
Prix Fixe: 280 francs
($56), lunch

RESTAURANTS BY NEIGHBORHOOD

The following is a select group of restaurants listed by *arrondissement*, so you can find good choices near your hotel. They are all *très français* and *très populaire*, and most of the clientele is French (in other words, these restaurants have not been overrun by tourists). The prices vary from inexpensive to *cher*. The *prix fixe* amount is listed when applicable, and in some cases the price range is included in the description. (American-style restaurants are listed on page 63.)

The First Arrondissement

L'ABSINTHE

This trendy spot is well located just off Rue St.-Honoré. The food is good, though not gourmet, and the prices are *pas donné* ("not given"— meaning expensive).

24 Place du Marché-St.-Honoré
Phone: 42–61–03–32
Métro: Tuileries
Cards: AE, MC, V

LE GRAND VEFOUR

In the 1960s and 1970s, Le Grand Véfour was *the* place to be seen in Paris, and celebrities flocked to this elegant oasis just off the beautiful gardens of Palais Royal. Today this is a wonderful hideaway to take your sweetheart, but be prepared for high prices.

17 Rue de Beaujolais
Phone: 42–96–56–27
Métro: Palais-Royal
Cards: AE, MC, V
Prix Fixe: 305 francs
($61), lunch

LOUIS XIV

Louis XIV is frequented by a chic crowd that is drawn by the great location. Place des Victoires is one of the prime shopping areas in Paris, circled by great designer shops.

1 Bis, Place des
  Victoires
Phone: 40–26–20–81
Métro: Bourse
Cards: AE, MC, V
Prix Fixe: 300 francs
($60), lunch

CHEZ PAULINE

This restaurant is popular for its good, classic French food. Chef André Genin is charming. He and Michel Rostang (see page 91) also have a French restaurant in Los Angeles called Fennel; they commute back and forth.

5 Rue Villedo
Phone: 42–96–20–70
Métro: Palais-Royal
Cards: AE, MC, V
Prix Fixe: 190 francs
($38), lunch

Chez Pauline.

PIERRE AU PALAIS-ROYAL

This is an intimate neighborhood meeting place that serves very simple, classic French dishes.

10 Rue de Richelieu
Phone: 42–96–09–17
Métro: Palais-Royal
Cards: MC, V
Prix Fixe: 220 francs
　($44), lunch and
　dinner

The Fourth Arrondissement

BOFINGER

Founded in 1864, Bofinger is reputed to be the oldest brasserie in Paris. The specialty of the house is *fruits de mer* (fresh shellfish), and there is always a crowd.

5 Rue de la Bastille
Phone: 42–72–87–82
Métro: Bastille
Cards: AE, MC, V
Prix Fixe: 155 francs
　($31), lunch and
　dinner

The Sixth Arrondissement

AUX CHARPENTIERS

This is a find! The decor is simple and cozy—lots of wood, old photos, and fresh flowers. The food is also simple and excellent, including a good selection of salads. The prices are reasonable. Our lunch for three totaled $87.

10 Rue Mabillon
Phone: 43–26–30–05
Métro: Mabillon
Cards: AE, MC, V

POLIDOR

Polidor's prices are a bargain (around $15 per person). While neighboring restaurants are half-empty, this place is hopping, with a waiting line extending onto the sidewalk. Diners are seated next to each other at long tables. The menu is simple and good and an excellent value.

41 Rue Monsieur le
　Prince
Phone: 43–26–95–34
Métro: Odéon or
　Luxembourg
Cards: None

LE TEMPS PERDU

Named "the lost time," this former horse stable is 400 years old. Today, it is popular with writers and serves traditional cuisine.

54 Rue de Seine
Phone: 46–34–12–08
Métro: St.-Germain-
　des-Prés or Odéon
Cards: AE, MC, V

Deciphering a French Menu

Now the fun begins. Deciphering a French menu (that doesn't have the English translations) is a herculean task. Some waiters speak a smattering of English, but you are likely to find yourself on your own. Since I suggest dining in neighborhood restaurants, off the beaten tourist track, you will definitely need some help in understanding what dishes are offered. The following two lists give the French/English translations for many of the basic terms. *Bonne chance!*

Je voudrais voir la carte.	I would like to see the menu.
Avez-vous choisi?	Have you decided?
L'addition, s'il vous plaît.	The check, please.
Service compris.	Service included (15 percent).

French/English

Addition. Bill.
Ananas. Pineapple.
Artichaut. Artichoke.
Asperge. Asparagus.
Assiette. Plate.
Avocat. Avocado.
Beurre. Butter.
Bifteck. Steak.
  Saignant. Rare.
  A point. Medium.
  Bien cuit. Well done.
Boissons. Drinks.
Brioche. Buttery roll.
Café. Coffee.*
Canard. Duck.
Carte. Menu.
Champignon. Mushroom.
Citron. Lemon.
Coquillages. Shellfish.
Côte d'agneau. Lamb chop.

Crème fraîche. Thick, sour, heavy cream.
Crudités. Raw vegetables.
Déjeuner. Lunch.
Dîner. Dinner, to dine.
Entrecôte. Beef rib steak.
Entrée. First course.
Fromage. Cheese.
Gâteau. Cake.
Glace. Ice cream.
Haricot vert. Green bean.
Jambon. Ham.
Jus. Juice.
Lait. Milk.
Légume. Vegetable.
Oeuf. Egg.

Pain. Bread.
Pamplemousse. Grapefruit.
Pêche. Peach.
Plat. A dish.
Poisson. Fish.
Poivre. Pepper.
Pomme. Apple.
Pomme de terre. Potato
Potage. Soup.
Poulet. Chicken.
Raisin. Grape.
Reçu. Receipt.
Saumon. Salmon.
Sel. Salt.
Serviette. Napkin.
Thé. Tea.*
Thon. Tuna fish.
Veau. Veal.
Viande. Meat.

English/French

Apple. *Pomme.*
Artichoke. *Artichaut.*
Asparagus. *Asperge.*
Avocado. *Avocat.*
Beef rib steak.
 Entrecôte.
Bill, check. *Addition.*
Bread. *Pain.*
Butter. *Beurre.*
Buttery roll. *Brioche.*
Cake. *Gâteau.*
Cheese. *Fromage.*
Chicken. *Poulet.*
Coffee. *Café.**
Cold Cuts. *Char-*
 cuteries.
Dinner, to dine.
 Dîner.
Dish. *Plat.*
Drinks. *Boissons.*

Duck. *Canard.*
Egg. *Oeuf.*
First course. *Entrée.*
Fish. *Poisson.*
Grape. *Raisin.*
Grapefruit.
 Pamplemousse.
Green bean. *Haricot*
 vert.
Ham. *Jambon.*
Ice cream. *Glace.*
Juice. *Jus.*
Lamb chop. *Côte*
 d'agneau.
Lemon. *Citron.*
Lunch. *Déjeuner.*
Meat. *Viande.*
Menu. *Carte.*
Milk. *Lait.*

Mushroom. *Cham-*
 pignon.
Napkin. *Serviette.*
Peach. *Pêche.*
Pepper. *Poivre.*
Pineapple. *Ananas.*
Plate. *Assiette.*
Potato. *Pomme de*
 terre.
Salmon. *Saumon.*
Salt. *Sel.*
Shellfish. *Coquillages.*
Soup. *Potage.*
Steak. *Bifteck.*
Rare. *Saignant.*
Medium. *A point.*
Well done. *Bien cuit.*
Tea. *Thé.**
Tuna fish. *Thon.*
Veal. *Veau.*

* A complete listing and explanation of coffee and tea terms is on page 85.

The Seventh Arrondissement

JULES VERNE

Jules Verne is one of the most romantic spots in Paris, with a stunning view of the city. The service and food are excellent. The *prix fixe* lunch is very reasonable for a once-in-a-lifetime experience.

Eiffel Tower, second level
On Champ-de-Mars
Phone: 45–55–61–44
Métro: Ecole-Militaire
Cards: AE, MC, V
Prix Fixe: 250 francs ($50), lunch

The Eighth Arrondissement

LE BOEUF SUR LE TOIT

This Art Déco brasserie specializes in seafood and caters to businessmen, artists, and models.

34 Rue du Colisée
Phone: 43–59–83–80
Métro: St.-Philippe-du-
  Roule
Cards: AE, MC, V

CHEZ ANDRE

Chez André is located in a great neighborhood with a great crowd and simple fare. Tables are packed closely together.

12 Rue Marbeuf
Phone: 47–20–59–57
Métro: Franklin-D.-
  Roosevelt
Cards: AE, MC, V

CHEZ FRANCIS

The highlight of this restaurant is sitting on the outdoor terrace adjacent to the Seine River facing the Eiffel Tower.

7 Rue Place de L'Alma
Phone: 47–20–86–83
Métro: Alma-Marceau
Cards: AE, MC, V
Prix Fixe: 200 francs
  ($40), lunch and
  dinner

The Tenth Arrondissement

BRASSERIE FLO

This quintessential Parisian brasserie is always bustling with patrons. It is off the beaten track, but worth the cab fare for the people-watching and the classic cuisine.

7 Cour des Petites-
  Ecuries
Phone: 47–70–13–59
Métro: Château-d'Eau
Cards: AE, MC, V
Prix Fixe: 95 francs
  ($19), lunch

The Fourteenth Arrondissement

LA CAGOUILLE

Chef Gérard Allemandou prepares delicious fish dishes, the specialty *de la maison* (of the house). He's already earning raves, so reserve ahead.

10-12 Place Constantin-
  Brancusi
Phone: 43–22–09–01
Métro: Gaité
Cards: MC, V

The Fifteenth Arrondissement

AUX TROIS CHEVRONS

A French friend took me here and asked me to keep this wonderful discovery a secret. Some secrets are meant to be shared. Every dish was mouth watering, and the menu changes daily. Best of all, the prices are half of what you would pay for an equivalent meal in the better-known restaurants. Our dinner was $35 per person, not counting wine.

148 Avenue Félix-Faure
Phone: 45–54–12–26
Métro: Balard
Cards: MC, V

The Sixteenth Arrondissement

BRASSERIE STELLA

Smack in the middle of the *seizième* (16th), this is the neighborhood haunt for the preppy inhabitants of the area.

133 Avenue Victor Hugo
Phone: 47–27–60–54
Métro: Victor Hugo
Cards: AE, MC, V

LES JARDINS DE BAGATELLE ♥

Bagatelle Park is a restful retreat. The rose gardens are beautiful, and the restaurant is surrounded by woods. If you are in Paris the second weekend of September, this is definitely the place to go. At that time, the most prestigious car show in the world is held at Bagatelle, and Les Jardins serves a special "Menu Automobiles Classiques" to the jet-set crowd in attendance.

Parc de Bagatelle
In Bois de Boulogne
Phone: 40–67–98–29
Métro: Not accessible
Cards: MC, V

PARIS LE 16

The simple menu is very reasonably priced, and the small dining room is lively and cozy, with diners seated next to each other at long tables.

18 Rue des Belles-Feuilles
Phone: 47–04–56–33
Métro: Trocadéro
Cards: None

Does a Café Differ From a Brasserie?

Just as we have diners, coffee shops, and restaurants, the French have several different kinds of places to eat. Here is a brief description of each.

Bistro. This is a casual, neighborhood spot, usually run by a husband-and-wife team. The small menu is written on a blackboard, and the *bistro* is frequented by regulars, *les habitués*.

Brasserie. *Brasserie* means brewery, and, as you might expect, *brasseries* boast good selections of beer and wine. The food is complementary to the beer, specializing in *charcuteries* (pork and other types of meat), and the menu is simple. The atmosphere is very lively and boisterous.

Café. *Cafés* vary in formality. Generally, they offer drinks and light meals. If there are two floors, the second level is usually more elaborate, with tablecloths and a wider menu.

Restaurant. The word restaurant originated from a thick soup that "restored" the appetite. Now, an elegant restaurant does much more than restore—it is a perfect setting for the celebration and enjoyment of life's finer pleasures on a grand scale.

WINE BARS

Wine bars originated in England in the 1970s and quickly became the rage in Paris. Normally, you can choose from over three dozen wines by the glass, and light meals are served. The French believe that wine should be enjoyed with food to complement the wine and bring out its full flavor. Wine bars (*bars à vins*) are lively, and great places to meet the French.

The First Arrondissement

WILLI'S WINE BAR   ♥

I love this place. The wines by the glass are delicious. The atmosphere is warm and friendly. The rustic wood decor is inviting, and, because the owner is British, the staff speaks excellent English. Lunch and dinner are served in the small adjoining dining room; it's best to reserve a table in advance. Afterwards, you can take a stroll through nearby Palais Royal.

13 Rue des Petits-
Champs
Phone: 42–61–05–09
Métro: Pyramides
Cards: MC, V

The Fifth Arrondissement

CAFE DE LA NOUVELLE MAIRIE

Adjacent to the Luxembourg Gardens, this café is in a lovely neighborhood. Light meals are served, but dinner service stops by 9:00 P.M.

19 Rue des Fossés-St.-Jacques
Phone: 43–26–80–18
Métro: Luxembourg
Cards: AE, MC, V

The Sixth Arrondissement

LE PETIT BACCHUS

Englishman Steven Spurrier founded this shop, which caters to serious wine lovers. The space is small—a half-dozen bar stools, with lots of wine bottles lining the walls. Only lunch is served, and closing time is around 8:00 P.M.

13 Rue du Cherche-Midi
Phone: 45–44–01–07
Métro: Sèvres-Babylone
Cards: MC, V

The Eighth Arrondissement

BLUE FOX BAR

The chic neighborhood draws a high-fashion crowd. A variety of salads is served. (This is located in a passageway off the street.)

25 Rue Royale
Phone: 42–65–10–72
Métro: Madeleine
Cards: MC, V

Baguettes

Baguettes are a staple of the French diet. During the day, you will see many people on the street carrying their daily fresh-baked, crusty *baguettes* home for the evening meal. They are also eaten as a morning snack—a *tartine* is a *baguette* sliced in half lengthwise and spread with lots of butter. *Baguettes* are also eaten at lunch time (*déjeuner*) with cheese and ham as sandwiches.

STREET MARKETS

One of the most fun and inexpensive ways to enjoy French cuisine is to put together a picnic lunch from an outdoor market. Big stands are overflowing with various kinds of produce, ripe fruit, and long-stemmed flowers, and everything looks so fresh you have the impression it was brought in from the farm that morning. Alongside the street are vendors offering everything from wine and cheese, to fresh-baked goods, to fish and meats. The *charcuteries* (similar to delicatessens) near these *marchés* (markets) offer delicious prepared foods.

"Daily marketing is still the rule in Paris, where everything from Camembert to cantaloupe is sold to be eaten that day, preferably within a few hours."
—*Patricia Wells*
The Food Lover's Guide to Paris

The street markets are normally open Tuesday through Saturday from 9:00 A.M. to 1:00 P.M., and then from 4:00 P.M. to 7:00 P.M. They are also open Sunday mornings.

RUE CLER
7th *arrondissement*
Starts at Avenue de la Motte-Picquet
Métro: Ecole-Militaire

RUE DE SEINE/BUCI   ♥
6th *arrondissement*
Starts at Boulevard St.-Germain
Métro: St.-Germain-des-Prés or Odéon

RUE DES BELLES-FEUILLES
16th *arrondissement*
Starts at Avenue Victor-Hugo
Métro: Victor-Hugo

GOURMET AND SPECIALTY STORES

Wandering through Paris' specialty stores is a delightful, entertaining, and delicious way to spoil yourself. These are excellent places to pick up inexpensive gifts—not perishable items, which aren't admitted into the United States when you go through customs. At Fauchon, I bought acrylic salt grinders, lovely ceramic jars, and passion tea.

The gourmet food shops of Paris are world renowned. Many of my friends make it a point to stop by Berthillon's ice cream shop on Ile Saint-Louis, even though the waiting line normally stretches around the block. Every food connoisseur is able to satisfy his or her whims in Paris.

In this section, the heart ♥ rating marks shops that are unforgettable experiences.

BERTHILLON (ICE CREAM)

This shop makes the most famous ice cream in Paris. There are dozens of flavors. The *glace*, ice cream, is more like a fruit sorbet than the creamy American variety.

31 Rue St.-Louis-en-l'Ile
Phone: 43–54–31–61
4th *arrondissement*
Métro: Pont-Marie

Berthillon.

Fauchon.

FAUCHON   ♥

This store is definitely a must-see. There is an unbelievable array of gourmet foodstuffs from all over the world. The complex is housed in two buildings. The first offers gourmet take-out, wines, and cheeses. The second building has two stores: one devoted to pastry, chocolate, and candy; the other housing a huge selection of packaged goods, from tea and coffee to condiments and dishes. This is wonderful for gift shopping—and they have a shipping service.

26 Place de la
  Madeleine
Phone: 47–42–60–11
8th *arrondissement*
Métro: Madeleine
Cards: AE, MC, V

FLO-PRESTIGE (TAKE-OUT)

This is a great place to shop for take-out items. From salad and breads to cheeses and salmon, everything is available in single servings. Flo-Prestige is open seven days a week until 11:00 P.M., so you can also get a late-night snack.

42 Place du Marché-
St.-Honoré
Phone: 42–61–45–46
1st *arrondissement*
Métro: Opéra or
Pyramides
Cards: AE, MC, V

GUENMAI (HEALTH FOOD)

This health-food store carries cereals, juices, vitamins, and many other natural products.

6 Rue Cardinale
Phone: 43–26–03–24
6th *arrondissement*
Métro: St.-Germain-
des-Prés
Cards: MC, V

HEDIARD

Hediard is near Fauchon, on the other side of Place de la Madeleine. Specialties include teas, coffees, spices, and items for the kitchen.

21 Place de la
Madeleine
Phone: 42–66–44–36
8th *arrondissement*
Métro: Madeleine
Cards: AE, MC, V

LES HERBES DU LUXEMBOURG

Les Herbes offers a great assortment of organic foods, fruits, nuts, and herbs.

3 Rue de Médicis
Phone: 43–26–91–53
6th *arrondissement*
Métro: Odéon or
Luxembourg
Cards: MC, V

LENOTRE (CHOCOLATES AND PASTRY) ♥

Gaston Lenôtre has become a legend for his chocolates and exquisite desserts. His design and presentation is a work of art, and you can pick up interesting gifts here.

49 Avenue Victor-Hugo
Phone: 45–01–71–71
16th *arrondissement*
Métro: Victor-Hugo
Cards: AE, MC, V
44 Rue du Bac
Phone: 42–22–39–39
7th *arrondissement*
Métro: Rue du Bac

LIONEL POILANE (BREAD)

Lionel Poilâne's fresh-baked bread could be a meal in and of itself—the variety and textures are so good. That is probably why it's sold at more than 600 shops around Paris and flown daily to other parts of the world.

8 Rue du Cherche-Midi
Phone: 45–48–42–59
6th *arrondissement*
Métro: Sèvres-Babylone

PETROSSIAN (CAVIAR)

This shop specializes in caviar, salmon, *foie gras*, and truffles.

18 Boulevard de la
  Tour-Maubourg
Phone: 45–51–59–73
7th *arrondissement*
Métro: Invalides
Cards: MC, V

SOLEIL DE PROVENCE (OLIVES)   ♥

Paul Tardieu ships the olives, herbs, honey, soap, and other products to the store from his farm in Provence—a sunny rural region in the south of France. Many of the items are very reasonably priced (under $10).

6 Rue du Cherche-Midi
Phone: 45–48–15–02
6th *arrondissement*
Métro: Sèvres-Babylone
Cards: None

Soleil de Provence.

COOKING CLASSES

An afternoon cooking class with *dégustation* (tasting) is a memorable way to learn about French cuisine firsthand. Many of the cooking schools conduct their classes in French, so you will want to make sure they provide a translator. Courses range in length from one afternoon to weeks or months. The top chefs suggest Robert Noah's Paris en Cuisine for its close-up glimpse of French cuisine. Mr. Noah, an American, offers tours of the top restaurants' kitchens, the food *marchés*, and the specialty shops.

Here are three options. You need to call in advance to make reservations.

LE CORDON BLEU

Founded in 1895, this is a very famous and traditional cooking school. The setting is not as elegant as the Ritz, and the school is geared to provide courses much longer than an afternoon's demonstration. English translators are provided on request.

8 Rue Léon-Delhomme
Phone: 48–56–06–06
15th *arrondissement*
Métro: Vaugirard
Cards: MC, V
Cost: 140 francs ($28)

PARIS EN CUISINE

Robert Noah arranges afternoon cooking demonstrations for small groups in some of the best restaurants in Paris. Naturally, they are topped off by a *dégustation*. Mr. Noah also organizes trips to the food *marchés*.

49 Rue de Richelieu
Phone: 42–61–35–23
1st *arrondissement*
Métro: Palais-Royal
Cost: 300 francs ($60), demonstration
Prefers payment in francs

RITZ COOKING SCHOOL

The Ritz cooking school is an elegant affair. Run by American Gregory Usher, the afternoon class lasts two and a half hours and includes a demonstration and tasting. You should reserve a day ahead.

38 Rue Cambon
Phone: 42–60–38–30
1st *arrondissement*
Métro: Concorde or Madeleine
Cards: AE, MC, V
Cost: 220 francs ($44)

Dining in Paris is a wonderful way to partake in the French culture firsthand and to have a great time doing it! You'll learn about many new dishes, and you may even get ideas for your own dinner parties. During one of my trips, I bought a French/English cookbook. Created by the staff of the American Hospital in Paris, this book contains some of my favorite recipes. The gourmet food and kitchen stores carry special items to add to your own cupboard or to give to friends so they, too, can enjoy a taste of Paris.

7. Les Boutiques

Splurge in the Most Fashionable Shops in the World

The French fashion world has been entertaining the rest of the world for decades. Each season, reporters arrive from distant lands to attend the *haute couture* designer shows and relay the latest styles and trends to their readers back home. Will the hemlines be above the knee or below? Are shoulder pads in or out? What colors are *de rigueur*?

Outside the show rooms, the streets of Paris are a show in and of themselves. French women enjoy and place great value on pulling together an elegant yet individual look. This is an art form that has been passed from mother to daughter for generations. And men get into the act too. Talk of fashion is as important in the French culture as politics and cuisine. Everyone has an opinion.

This chapter explores the most fashionable streets to stroll, lists the top *couture* houses, tells you how to obtain an invitation to a fashion show, discusses the best department stores, points the way to finding bargains, guides you in the art of choosing accessories, and explains customs regulations. There are also shopping tips, a glimpse at the most fashionable streets to stroll, and a size conversion chart.

Throughout the chapter, the heart ♥ rating indicates my top choices.

"Instinctive style is a particularly French quality, one that does not exist by accident or without historical references. . . . important French ladies of the seventeenth and eighteenth centuries used their personal eccentricities to influence all the courts of Europe. An original, noticeable [fashion] mode was considered as essential as writing fascinating letters, commissioning masterpieces by the right composers and painters, or pushing for advantageous treaties, alliances, or boycotts. Powerful French females always had powerful styles."
—*Marian McEvoy*
European Travel & Life

TOP COUTURE HOUSES

In *haute couture*, the epitome of French style, clothes are made *sur mesure* (by measure), meaning that each garment is custom-made. Top designers present their new creations twice a year, in January and in June, at elaborate fashion shows attended by celebrities, journalists, and customers willing to pay $30,000 for a unique, perfectly fitted gown. Guests are presented with a list of the garments to be modeled so that they can mark the items they may want to purchase. It is estimated that there are less than 2,500 serious *couture* customers left in the world.

After the premiere of a collection, it is possible to obtain an invitation to some of the shows. One method is to ask your hotel concierge to reserve a seat; or, you can call the house directly. After the first few weeks of previews with models, the house shows a videotape to prospective customers.

Two of the top French department stores, Galeries Lafayette and Printemps, offer year-round fashion shows in English. If you've missed the *couture* shows, these are the next best thing. There is no charge, but you do need to call or write ahead to reserve a place (for addresses and phone numbers, see page 112).

Prêt à porter, meaning "ready to wear," is a wonderful development for those of us who don't want to spend our life's savings on one dress. The *prêt à porter* clothes are similar in design and style to *haute couture*, but are mass-produced and sold "off-the-rack" in boutiques at one-tenth the *couture* price. Many *couture* houses offer a *prêt à porter* line.

A Know Your Size chart with French/English size conversions for women's and men's clothes and shoes can be found on page 110. Here is a listing of many of the top names in fashion.

BALMAIN
44 Rue François-Premier
Phone: 47–20–35–34
8th *arrondissement*
Métro: Franklin-D.-Roosevelt
Cards: AE, MC, V

CHANEL ♥
42 Avenue Montaigne
Phone: 47–23–74–12
8th *arrondissement*
Métro: Franklin-D.-Roosevelt
Cards: AE, MC, V

CHRISTIAN DIOR ♥
30 Avenue Montaigne
Phone: 40–73–54–44
8th *arrondissement*
Métro: Franklin-D.-Roosevelt
Cards: AE, MC, V

CHRISTIAN LACROIX
73 Rue du Faubourg-St.-Honoré
Phone: 42–65–79–08
8th *arrondissement*
Métro: Miromesnil
Cards: AE, MC, V

EMANUEL UNGARO
2 Avenue Montaigne
Phone: 47–23–61–94
8th *arrondissement*
Métro: Alma-Marceau
 or Franklin-D.-Roosevelt
Cards: AE, MC, V

GIVENCHY
3 Avenue George-V
Phone: 47–23–81–36
8th *arrondissement*
Métro: George-V
Cards: AE, MC, V

GUY LAROCHE
30 Rue du Faubourg-St.-Honoré
Phone: 42–65–62–74
8th *arrondissement*
Métro: Concorde or Madeleine
Cards: AE, MC, V

JEAN-LOUIS SCHERRER
51 Avenue Montaigne
Phone: 43–59–55–39
8th *arrondissement*
Métro: Franklin-D.-Roosevelt
Cards: AE, MC, V

KARL LAGERFELD
19 Rue du Faubourg-St.-Honoré
Phone: 42–66–64–64
8th *arrondissement*
Métro: Concorde
Cards: AE, MC, V

LANVIN
22 Rue du Faubourg-St.-Honoré
Phone: 42–65–14–40
8th *arrondissement*
Métro: Concorde
Cards: AE, MC, V

LOUIS FERAUD
88 Rue du Faubourg-St.-Honoré
Phone: 42–65–27–29
8th *arrondissement*
Métro: Champs-Elysées-Clémenceau
Cards: AE, MC, V

NINA RICCI
39 Avenue Montaigne
Phone: 47–23–78–88
8th *arrondissement*
Métro: Franklin-D.-Roosevelt
Cards: AE, MC, V

PIERRE CARDIN
27 Avenue Marigny
Phone: 42–66–92–25
8th *arrondissement*
Métro: Champs-Elysées-Clémenceau
Cards: AE, MC, V

SONIA RYKIEL
70 Rue du Faubourg-St.-Honoré
Phone: 42–65–20–81
8th *arrondissement*
Métro: Concorde
Cards: AE, MC, V

VALENTINO
17-19 Avenue Montaigne
Phone: 47–23–64–61
8th *arrondissement*
Métro: Alma-Marceau
 or Franklin-D.-Roosevelt
Cards: AE, MC, V

**YVES SAINT LAURENT-
RIVE GAUCHE ♥**
38 Rue du Faubourg-St.-Honoré
Phone: 42–65–74–59
8th *arrondissement*
Métro: Concorde
Cards: AE, MC, V

Know Your Size

The following conversion charts will help you find clothes and shoes in your size. There is some variation, so you will still need to try things on for fit, but at least you'll be in the ballpark. The French translations for basic English clothing terms are in parentheses underneath each heading.

There are two words for size in French: *taille* is used for clothes, and *pointure* refers to shoes and gloves.

Women's Dresses, Coats, and Skirts
(robes, manteaux, and jupes)

American	3	5	7	9	11	12	13	14	15	16	18
French	36	38	38	40	40	42	42	44	44	46	48

Women's Blouses and Sweaters
(blouses, pullovers)

American	10	12	14	16	18	20
French	38	40	42	44	46	48

Women's Shoes
(chaussures femmes)

American	5	6	7	8	9	10
French	36	37	38	39	40	41

Men's Suits
(complets)

American	34	36	38	40	42	44	46	48
French	44	46	48	50	52	54	56	58

Men's Shirts
(chemises)

American	14½	15	15½	16	16½	17	17½	18
French	37	38	39	41	42	43	44	45

Men's Shoes
(chaussures hommes)

American	7	8	9	10	11	12	13
French	39½	41	42	43	44½	46	47

Fashionable Stree

Most of the top designers have a number o...
However, the following four areas are especially...
window-shopping, and mingling with the *crème* of Pa...

- The Avenue Montaigne—in the 8th *arrondissement*, be...
  Champs-Elysées and the Seine River—exemplifies elegance and ...
  host to Christian Dior, Nina Ricci, Valentino, and Chanel, among
  others.
- The Rue St.-Honoré, starting in the 1st *arrondissement* and continu-
  ing into the 8th *arrondissement,* is the longest-running street of top
  stores in Paris, stretching well over a mile.
- Place des Victoires is a picturesque circle of avant-garde boutiques
  located a few blocks from the Louvre at the intersection with Rue des
  Petits-Champs.
- The Boulevard St.-Germain, in the 6th *arrondissement,* is part of a tri-
  angle of smaller boutiques whose other two boundaries are formed by
  Rue de Rennes and Rue du Four. This is my favorite area, and also
  comes highly recommended by my Parisian girlfriends. ♥

Christian Dior boutique

...RTMENT STORES

...discussion of Paris department stores, you need know only two
...s: Galeries Lafayette. There is a handful of good department stores in
...s, but Galeries Lafayette has the widest selection—110 departments in
...o adjacent buildings—and carries all the top designer clothes, shoes,
...ccessories, lingerie, you name it.

Galeries Lafayette also caters to Americans. Many of the salespeople
speak English, and if you spend over 2,000 francs ($400), you can obtain a
form to have the 13-to-18-percent sales tax, *détaxe*, reimbursed (more on
this on page 120). The store's size is a bit intimidating, but this is definitely
the place for one-stop shopping.

In addition to the four major department stores listed here, there are
two discount department store chains—Prisunic and Monoprix—with out-
lets throughout Paris. Their bargain prices for casual clothing, accessories,
and many other goods make them very popular with Parisians for simple
purchases. Rumor has it that even Princess Caroline has gone to these
stores for a quick addition to her wardrobe.

BON MARCHE

The oldest department store in Paris, Bon Marché
carries top fashion designs and trendy new labels.

38 Rue de Sèvres
Phone: 45–49–21–22
7th *arrondissement*
Métro: Sèvres-Babylone
Cards: AE, MC, V

GALERIES LAFAYETTE ♥

Galeries Lafayette—the biggest Paris department
store—offers fashion shows one or two days a
week year-round. Call ahead to reserve a seat.

40 Boulevard Haussmann
Phone: 48–74–02–30
9th *arrondissement*
Métro: Chaussée-
   d'Antin or Opéra
Cards: AE, MC, V

PRINTEMPS

Located across the street from Galeries Lafayette,
Printemps, like its rival, offers fashion shows twice
a week.

64 Boulevard Haussmann
Phone: 42–82–50–00
9th *arrondissement*
Métro: Chaussée-
   d'Antin or Opéra
Cards: AE, MC, V

Galeries Lafayette.

AUX TROIS QUARTIERS

This store has an extensive *couture* collection as well as a big selection of hair accessories and hats.

10 Boulevard de la
Madeleine
Phone : 42–60–39–30
1st *arrondissement*
Métro: Madeleine
Cards: AE, MC, V

DESIGNER OUTLETS

While browsing on Avenue Montaigne and Rue du Faubourg-St.-Honoré, you may be struck by the high price tags. Fear not. There are shops with designer labels at discount prices. The surroundings and service may not be as elegant as those of the *haute couture* houses, but you'll be pleased with the savings. Be forewarned, though: some shops don't accept credit cards.

ANNA LOWE

Prices here start at 25 percent off the original cost. The shop carries all sizes, including some models' samples in sizes 6 and 8.

35 Avenue Matignon
Phone: 45–63–45–57
8th *arrondissement*
Métro: Miromesnil
Cards: AE, MC, V

BABS

Babs carries Guy Laroche *couture* and other labels in *prêt à porter*.

29 Avenue Marceau
Phone: 47–20–84–74
16th *arrondissement*
Métro: Charles-de-
Gaulle-Etoile
Cards: AE, MC, V

BOUTIQUE DE SOLDES

Here, you'll find Jean-Louis Scherrer and other designer labels.

29 Avenue Ledru-Rollin
Phone: 46–28–39–27
12th *arrondissement*
Métro: Gare de Lyon
Cards: None

MAXANDRE

In Maxandre, Valentino designs from previous collections are sold at a discount, and clothes from Valentino's current season are offered at their full price.

42 Rue du Faubourg-
St.-Honoré
Phone: 42–65–52–50
8th *arrondissement*
Métro: Concorde
Cards: AE, MC, V

Shopping Tips

Many shopkeepers speak some English since it's become the predominant language spoken with tourists in Paris. I'm always amazed to hear French salespeople speaking English with customers from Japan, Italy, Germany, you name it. The accents are from all over the map.

Still, some shopkeepers do not speak English. Also, as you'll discover on your first foray into stores, French shopping customs are somewhat different from ours. The following guidelines and phrases should help you to better enjoy *les boutiques.*

- Shopping hours vary, depending on the season. Stores are usually closed Sundays and holidays. Most stores open by 10:00 A.M. and close around 7:00 P.M., and many are closed during lunch time. August is the national month of vacation, so many stores close for a few weeks during this time.
- If you notice a sign in the window saying *Soldes*, that does not mean that all the merchandise has already been purchased. On the contrary, it means that items are on sale, and that you will save some francs. Normally, stores put their stock on sale twice a year, in January and in June.
- Many stores will reimburse the 13-to-18-percent sales tax if you buy more than 2,000 francs in merchandise at their store. Remember to get the Export Sales Invoice (see details on page 120).
- Some bigger stores will ship your purchases to the States for a small fee. Or you can go to the nearest post office and ship the goods yourself (for the addresses of two main post offices, see page 156). Most post offices sell various size boxes for this purpose. The least expensive method of shipment is by boat, which takes six weeks.

Common Phrases

How much does this cost?
Ça coûte combien?

Do you accept credit cards or traveler's checks?
Acceptez-vous les cartes de crédit ou les chèques de voyage?

I would like the Export Sales Invoice for sales tax reimbursement.
Je voudrais l'imprimé pour la détaxe.

I would like the package gift wrapped.
Je voudrais un paquet cadeau.

MENDES

Tried and true, this store comes highly recommended by many bargain shoppers. It carries a good selection of Yves Saint Laurent and other big names.

65 Rue Montmartre
Phone: 42–36–83–32
9th *arrondissement*
Métro: Les Halles
Cards: MC, V

RECIPROQUE

Réciproque offers new and used clothes and designer samples. Many labels are represented here.

95 Rue de la Pompe
Phone: 47–04–30–28
16th *arrondissement*
Métro: Pompe
Cards: MC, V

Accessories

French women play at creating different moods by mixing and matching their belts and scarves and shoes and purses, and by adding fun jewelry. *Les accessoires* (the accessories) give the French an inexpensive way to jazz up their outfits and showcase their originality and personality. Expermentation and trying the unexpected have been developed to a fine art.

Here, again, Galeries Lafayette is a good place to start, because it offers a wide array of every type of accessory imaginable. The following is a sampling of smaller boutiques. Many of these stores have branches in other locations. They all accept credit cards.

"The French look consists of a variety of styles but a single spirit—self expression. And nowhere is it more evident than in a Frenchwoman's accessories, in the details that finish, but more often fashion, the entire outfit. Frenchwomen wear clever accessories, which they change at whim to instantly update any old thing and give it the stamp of originality. They seem to have an implicit understanding of the little touches needed to achieve just the effect they want."
—*Susan Sommers
French Chic*

SHOES AND PURSES

French women consider shoes a mainstay of their wardrobe, and shoe designers are as well known and coveted as their *couture* counterparts. What's most important is that shoes be well made with good leather in strong, basic colors. The purse doesn't have to match, but it should be complementary.

CAREL
4 Rue Tronchet
Phone: 42–66–21–58
8th *arrondissement*
Métro: Madeleine

CHARLES JOURDAN
5 Boulevard de la Madeleine
Phone: 42–65–35–22
1st *arrondissement*
Métro: Madeleine

DIDIER LAMARTHE ♥
19 Rue de l'Echaudé
Phone: 43–29–47–03
6th *arrondissement*
Métro: St.-Germain-des-Prés

Shoes are not sold here, but you will find a gorgeous selection of purses and other leather goods like suitcases and coin purses. The earthy colors and elegant designs are first-rate.

LAURENT MERCADEL
3 Place des Victoires
Phone: 45–08–84–44
2nd *arrondissement*
Métro: Bourse or Palais-Royal

MAUD FRIZON
83 Rue des Saints-Pères
Phone: 42–22–06–93
6th *arrondissement*
Métro: Sèvres-Babylone

ROBERT CLERGERIE
5 Rue du Cherche-Midi
Phone: 45–48–75–47
6th *arrondissement*
Métro: Rennes

STEPHANE KELIAN
6 Place des Victoires
Phone: 42–61–60–74
2nd *arrondissement*
Métro: Bourse

WALTER STEIGER
5 Rue de Tournon
Phone: 46–33–01–45
6th *arrondissement*
Métro: Odéon

SCARVES AND BELTS

Scarves are great accents to liven up and enhance your outfit and set off your face. Large scarves can also be worn as shawls over one shoulder.

The following stores are known for their scarf counters, but they sell many other items as well, including a variety of leather goods. Hermés scarves are a French trademark. Worn with a suit or jeans, they are an important part of the French woman's wardrobe.

CHRISTIAN DIOR ♥
30 Avenue Montaigne
Phone: 40–73–54–44
8th *arrondissement*
Métro: Franklin-D.-Roosevelt

GUCCI
35 Rue du Faubourg-St.-Honoré
Phone: 42–96–83–27
1st *arrondissement*
Métro: Opéra

HERMES
24 Rue du Faubourg-St.-Honoré
Phone: 40–17–47–17
8th *arrondissement*
Métro: Concorde

LOUIS VUITTON
54 Avenue Montaigne
Phone: 45–62–47–00
8th *arrondissement*
Métro: Alma-Marceau
  or Franklin-D.-Roosevelt

JEWELRY

A stylish piece of jewelry is the finishing touch to add a note of glamour or formality—or just plain fun. It doesn't have to be expensive. I'm always picking up great bargains at the department store counters; there, you'll find big selections of costume jewelry for a wide range of prices. There are also whole boutiques devoted to *faux bijoux* (fake jewels). The three stores listed directly below are *très cher* and great for window-shopping or browsing with a rich boyfriend. Stores that carry wonderful collections of costume jewelry are listed on page 120.

Expensive Jewels (Vrai Bijoux)

CARTIER
7 Place Vendôme
Phone: 42–61–55–55
1st *arrondissement*
Métro: Tuileries or Opéra

FRED
6 Rue Royale
Phone: 42–60–30–65
8th *arrondissement*
Métro: Concorde

VAN CLEEF ET ARPELS
22 Place Vendôme
Phone: 42–61–58–58
1st *arrondissement*
Métro: Opéra

Cartier.

Shopping Escorts

Shopping escorts offer a valuable means of conserving your limited time and focusing your energies on the purchases you want to make. Chic Promenade is run by Maribeth Ricour de Bourgies, an American who moved to Paris and married a Frenchman. She offers five different types of shopping tours, each of which lasts a half day and includes a maximum of six people. The tours range in price from 250 francs per person for a walking tour to 2,900 francs for five people (580 francs each) for the Chic Promenade Privilege. For the latter tour, the group is escorted in a chauffeur-driven limousine to Paris' most elegant shopping districts, and the trip is custom-made to the group's tastes and desires.

Maribeth has also written an excellent shopping guide, *The Chic Shopper's Guide to Paris*, which is a good reference for all aspects of shopping.

CHIC PROMENADE
21 Bis, Rue Voltaire
Phone: 43–48–85–04
11th *arrondissement*

Costume Jewels (Faux Bijoux)

BURMA
16 Rue de la Paix
Phone: 42–61–60–64
2nd *arrondissement*
Métro: Opéra

72 Rue du Faubourg-St.-Honoré
Phone: 42–65–44–90
8th *arrondissement*
Métro: Miromesnil

FABRICE
54 Rue Bonaparte
Phone: 43–26–09–49
6th *arrondissement*
Métro: St.-Germain-des-Prés

P.F.T.
4 Rue Bernard-Palissy
Phone: 45–44–44–80
6th *arrondissement*
Métro: St.-Germain-des-Prés

REMINISCENCE
22 Rue du Four
Phone: 46–33–32–61
6th *arrondissement*
Métro: Mabillon

UTILILTY-BIBI BIJOUX
27 Rue du Four
Phone: 43–25–53–77
6th *arrondissement*
Métro: Mabillon

Customs

Applying for Sales Tax Reimbursement

To encourage tourists to shop, the French government has decreed that if you spend more than 2,000 francs at one store, the hefty 13-to-18–percent sales tax (depending on the category of the item), which is included in the price tag, will be reimbursed after you have left the country. In order to collect your money, you must do the following.

1. Get an Export Sales Invoice from each store at which you spend over the minimum 2,000 francs. Make sure you have three copies of the invoice. I was given only two by one store, and the airport customs official would not process my claim.
2. When you go to the airport, allow an extra hour to stop at the French Exit Customs office. First, they will ask to examine the goods you purchased. They will then keep one pink copy of the invoice, have you deposit the other pink copy in the mailbox next to their window, and give you the validated green copy as a receipt. The store will then be directed to send the money to the address you listed on the form, or to simply credit the charge card you indicated.
3. If you leave France by train, contact the car conductor, and he will collect the forms during the trip.

Fashion Through the Ages

The Musée de la Mode et du Costume displays one of the richest collections of fashion in the world. Over 5,000 complete costumes from the eighteenth century to the present day are housed in this Italian Renaissance palace. The long history of French elegance is depicted in royal evening robes and many articles of clothing that were donated by "*les belles dames de la haute société*" (the beautiful women of high society)—various countesses and princesses. This museum also hosts revolving exhibitions.

Palais Galliéra
10 Avenue Pierre-
 Premier-de-Serbie
Phone: 47–20–85–23
16th *arrondissement*
Métro: Iéna

Clearing United States Customs

When you return to the United States, you will have to fill out a Customs Declaration Form. If you purchased over $400 in goods, you will be asked to pay a 10-percent duty on any merchandise above that amount, up to $1,000. So, for example, if you bought $600 worth of clothes, you would pay 10-percent duty on $200, or $20. (A few items are exempt from customs' duty, including original works of art.) Above $1,400, the duty varies, depending on the item.

This process is easiest if you keep the receipts from all your purchases in your wallet and pack all your dutiable goods in one bag that's easy to retrieve.

I enjoy window-shopping and browsing through stores as much as actually buying things. The dollar's exchange rate against the franc is not very strong right now and prices are fairly high, so I tend to limit my purchases to less-expensive items, like separates I can mix and match, and unusual accessories. Shopkeepers in the smaller boutiques are usually more friendly and welcoming than the personnel in bigger stores, and if you engage the salespeople in conversation, they will be happy to share their advice and expertise.

8. Pour la Maison

Develop Your Decorating Style

A woman's guide to Paris wouldn't be complete without at least a brief mention of the many beautiful shops devoted to *la maison*, the house. The quality and fabulous selection of household items in Paris are superb. You may decide to purchase a small gift for a friend or buy an accessory to spruce up a room in your home.

This chapter will touch on museums that trace the history and evolution of home furnishings; antique stores; specialty boutiques; auctions; and flea markets. Yes, there are still finds to be had, and the following listings will give you many ideas for enhancing your environment and adding a new dimension to your decorating style.

"The French mix what they like with what they need with what the family has handed down. The look is eclectic and yet cohesive. The best of French country style is comfortable, graceful, and gracious—a mixture of color, texture, substance, and light that welcomes and charms in a way that is refreshingly open."
—Pierre Moulin,
Pierre Le Vec, and
Linda Dannenberg
Pierre Deux's
French Country

MUSEUMS

Paris has two museums devoted to home furnishings. Musée des Arts Decoratifs is a great place to start your exploration of French decorating style. Adjacent to the Louvre, and equally awesome in size, it contains four treasure-filled floors of exhibits, including a number of period rooms that recreate French interiors from the seventeenth century through the Art Déco period of this century. In addition to furniture, there are tapestries, sculpture, porcelains, silver, and jewelry. There is no other decorative museum of this scope in Europe.

The other museum is adjacent to the Baccarat store in the 10th *arrondissement*. Since 1764, Baccarat crystal has been sought by kings, presidents, and all those who could afford the high price tags. Baccarat still manufactures world-renowned designs, and its museum traces the history of crystal and displays the company's most historic pieces.

MUSEE DES ARTS DECORATIFS
107 Rue de Rivoli
Phone: 42–60–32–14
1st *arrondissement*
Métro: Palais-Royal

BACCARAT
30 Bis, Rue de Paradis
Phone: 47–70–64–30
10th *arrondissement*
Métro: Château d'Eau or Poissonnière

ANTIQUE STORES

Paris has thousands of antique and secondhand stores. Beware of the proliferation of forgeries, though. Your safest bet is to buy from established dealers who provide a certificate of authenticity. The Left Bank, or *Rive Gauche*, has a profusion of antique stores in one section: on Rue Bonaparte; from Boulevard St.-Germain to the Seine River; then west along the Quai to Rue de Beaune; and back towards Boulevard St.-Germain.

In addition to the many stores you'll find on the Left Bank, there are two major centers that house a number of antique dealers under one roof.

LE LOUVRE DES ANTIQUAIRES

Possibly the world's most popular antique center, Le Louvre des Antiquaires has something for everyone among the 250 dealers. Although the prices are rather steep, this is a great place to go, especially on a rainy day, because everything is housed under one roof.

2 Place du Palais-Royal
Phone: 42–97–27–00
1st *arrondissement*
Métro: Palais-Royal
Cards: AE, MC, V
Closed: Mondays

VILLAGE SUISSE

Named after the Swiss Pavilion of the 1889 World's Fair, this complex boasts over 100 shops.

56 Avenue de la Motte-Picquet at Avenue de Suffren
Phone: 43–06–69–90
7th *arrondissement*
Métro: La Motte-Picquet or Ecole-Militaire
Closed: Tuesdays and Wednesdays

Musée des Arts Decoratifs.

SPECIALTY BOUTIQUES FOR HOUSEHOLD ITEMS

The French love to entertain at home in style, and the selection and quality of boutiques for the house is a testament to this passion. French royalty enjoyed a very lavish lifestyle for centuries, and traces of that civilization linger on.

Artificial Flowers

TROUSSELIER

Trousselier has mastered the famous French craft of making silk flowers and flower arrangements that are more lovely than the real thing. This century-old shop has been owned by the same family for three generations.

73 Boulevard Haussman
Phone: 42–66–97–95
8th *arrondissement*
Métro: Havre-
  Caumartin
or Gare-St.-Lazare
Cards: AE, MC, V

The Bath

BEAUTE DIVINE

This shop offers a nostalgic collection of bathroom accessories from the 1930s, as well as contemporary towels, lamps, and accessories.

40 Rue St.-Sulpice
Phone: 43–26–25–31
6th *arrondissement*
Métro: Odéon
Cards: AE, MC, V

The Bed

LA BOUTIQUE DU SOMMEIL

In this boutique, all bedtime wishes are ful-
filled—nightgowns and pajamas, satin and raw-
silk sheets, and trays to serve breakfast in bed in
the morning.

24 Avenue Pierre-
Premier-de-Serbie
Phone: 47–20–57–36
16th *arrondissement*
Métro: Iéna
Cards: AE, MC, V

Carpets

A LA PLACE CLICHY

This shop carries a good selection of antique car-
pets and hand-crafted rugs in various sizes.

93 Rue d'Amsterdam
Phone: 45–26–15–16
8th *arrondissement*
Métro: Place Clichy
Cards: MC, V

China and Crystal

BACCARAT

Established in 1764, Baccarat still manufactures
world-renowned crystal designs.

30 Bis, Rue de Paradis
Phone: 47–70–64–30
10th *arrondissement*
Métro: Château-d'Eau
  or Poissonnière
Cards: AE, MC, V

CHRISTOFLE

This 100-year-old firm is *the* name in dinnerware
and fine porcelain. It carries exclusively the
Claude Monet and George Sand dinner services
(you need to order them three months in
advance).

17 Rue de Sèvres
Phone: 45–48–16–17
6th *arrondissement*
Métro: Sèvres-Babylone
Cards: AE, MC, V

9 Rue Royale
Phone: 49–33–43–00
8th *arrondissement*
Métro: Concorde

LALIQUE

Lalique is one of the world's foremost crystal
designers.

11 Rue Royale
Phone: 42–65–33–70
8th *arrondissement*
Métro: Concorde
Cards: AE, MC, V

LIMOGES-UNIC

In this shop, you'll find a good selection of various top brands of china, crystal, and table decorations.

12 Rue de Paradis
Phone: 47-70-54-49
10th *arrondissement*
Métro: Poissonnière
Cards: AE, MC, V

58 Rue de Paradis
Phone: 47-70-61-49
10th *arrondissement*
Métro: Château-d'Eau

LA PORCELAINE BLANCHE

Specializing in white porcelain, La Porcelaine Blanche offers discounts of 15 to 30 percent.

108 Rue St.-Honoré
Phone: 42-36-90-73
1st *arrondissement*
Métro: Louvre
Cards: MC, V

Dining

AU BAIN MARIE

Here, you'll find wonderful accessories and linen for your dining table, as well as cookbooks from all eras of cuisine.

10 Boissy d'Anglais
Phone: 42-66-59-74
8th *arrondissement*
Métro: Madeleine
Cards: AE, MC, V

DINERS EN VILLE

Because the quality of Diners en Ville's merchandise is so high and the store stocks everything for the dining room, many French women arrange their wedding registries here.

89 Rue du Bac
Phone: 42-22-78-33
7th *arrondissement*
Métro: Bac
Credit Cards: MC, V

Glassware

GALERIE D'AMON

Just off the Luxembourg Gardens, Galerie D'Amon carries *objets de décoration* and original art pieces at prices of 400 to 500 francs and up.

28 Rue St.-Sulpice
Phone: 43-26-96-60
6th *arrondissement*
Métro: Odéon
Cards: AE, MC, V

The Kitchen

CULINARION

Here, you'll find practical kitchen utensils in attractive styles.

99 Rue de Rennes
Phone: 45–48–94–76
6th *arrondissement*
Métro: Rennes
Cards: AE, MC, V

DEHILLERIN

Dehillerin carries every kind of pot and pan imaginable—mainly in copper, with some in stainless steel.

18 Rue Coquillière
Phone: 42–36–53–13
1st *arrondissement*
Métro: Châtelet-Halles
Cards: MC, V

Linens

PORTHAULT

Porthault specializes in luxurious raw-silk sheets and embroidered tablecloths. Prices here are *très cher*.

18 Avenue Montaigne
Phone: 47–20–75–25
8th *arrondissement*
Métro: Alma-Marceau
Cards: AE, MC, V

SOPHIE CANOVAS

The location alone is reason to shop at Canovas. Place Furstenberg is a well-kept secret among Parisians. The quality of the sheets, towels, tableclothes, and other accessories is superb, which is why the prices are so high.

5 Place Furstenberg
Phone: 43–26–89–31
6th *arrondissement*
Métro: St.-Germain-
   des-Prés
Cards: AE, MC, V

FLEA MARKETS

Known as *marchés aux puces*, flea markets first appeared in Paris in 1890 as a means of selling used clothing and bedding. The selection and quality of the goods has vastly improved since then. My Parisian friends have made valuable finds, including paintings, old watches, and antique furniture.

Flea markets are generally open Saturday, Sunday, and Monday, starting at 7:30 A.M. I'm told that it's best to show up early, before the good items are snatched up by professional antique hunters. Many vendors do not accept credit cards, so bring your francs, and be prepared to bargain on the prices. If you're good, the salesperson can be talked down.

How to Attend an Auction

There is one main auction house in Paris: Hôtel Drouot. Several auctions are held simultaneously, seven days a week, starting at 2:00 P.M. and running to 6:00 P.M. Anyone can attend, and everything is conducted in French. The prices range from a few dollars to a great many, *beaucoup*, and American checks are not accepted. Drouot is closed on weekends during the summer.

HOTEL DROUOT
9 Rue Drouot
9th *arrondissement*
Métro: Le Pelletier

The Flea Market at Saint-Ouen.

PORTE DE VANVES

A French friend who has found many good buys (including an old map he sold to Sotheby's for ten times what he paid) recommends Porte de Vanves. Open Saturday and Sunday, this is much smaller than Clignancourt. It takes only an hour or two to see everything, and the prices range from a few francs to *beaucoup*. The best time to go is Saturday morning.

Avenue Georges-Lafenestre
14th *arrondissement*
Métro: Porte de Vanves

SAINT-OUEN

Over 3,500 dealers display their wares at Saint-Ouen, which is the biggest flea market in the world. The 2,000 antique dealers have permanent stands, while another 1,500 dealers display their goods on tables or from the backs of cars and trucks. Prices range from a few dollars to astronomical figures for authenticated antiques. As you enter from Porte de Clignancourt, you need to walk past a few blocks of street vendors before you get to the real market.

Porte de Clignancourt
On Rue des Rosiers, starting at Avenue Michelet
18th *arrondissement*
Métro: Porte de Clignancourt

On every trip to Paris, I bring back souvenirs that stir warm memories of special experiences and reflect newly acquired tastes. Visitors to my home and office quickly see that I've been influenced by the French style.

You don't have to spend a lot of money to add charm, color, and a special flair to a room. Creating an inviting environment can be as simple as splurging on a beautiful vase and filling it with fresh flowers, buying a set of linen napkins to use when you're entertaining, or indulging in a scented candle that will add a woodsy aroma to your bedroom.

Good hunting!

9. Les Sports et Les Excursions

Enjoy the Great Outdoors

Attending a sporting event is one sure-fire way to gain close proximity to more Frenchmen than you can choose from. The team sports are different from our national pastimes, so you can innocently ask the adorable Frenchman seated next to you to explain the rules of the game, and pray that he speaks English. The most popular sport is French football, which is similar to soccer; members of the team, or *équipe*, are national celebrities. Car races, polo matches, and the French Open tennis tournament are also big draws, and the top French companies cosponsor these events.

One of the most grueling events is the annual Paris-Dakar race. Hundreds of contestants, competing in all manner of vehicles (motorcycles, cars, and jeeps), depart from Paris on Christmas morning and arrive three weeks later in the city of Dakar in Senegal, west Africa. Counted among my prize possessions are two silver bracelets given to me by a French beau who bought them in the middle of the African desert during the race.

Of course, if you're traveling with your boyfriend or husband, this chapter should be of particular interest, because it's all about sports. The section at the end describes idyllic parks and gardens where the two of you can while away an afternoon.

Depending on the season, there are many activities you can enjoy first-hand:

- Walking and jogging are the simplest forms of exercise, and you can't beat the scenery in Paris' exquisite gardens.
- French *gymnasiums*, the equivalent of our health clubs, are growing in popularity, although they still have a way to go to compete with *Jane Fonda's Workout*.

131

- In the heat of summer, the *piscines* (swimming pools) are a refreshing break.
- In addition to watching the tennis pros at Roland Garros Stadium, you can challenge a friend to a match at one of the local *stades*.
- Bicycling in the parks and surrounding countryside is a wonderful activity to share with a companion. Bring a picnic lunch, and you will create a scene reminiscent of an impressionist painting.

This chapter suggests three ways you can enjoy the great outdoors around Paris: attending a sporting event, engaging in your favorite sport, and spending a day at one of the beautiful gardens or parks. The heart ♥ rating indicates my top choices.

ATTENDING A SPORTING EVENT

Three weekly publications, *Pariscope*, *L'Officiel des Spectacles*, and *7 à Paris*, list all upcoming sports events. Since they are printed in French, you may need to ask for assistance in arranging your reservations.

Following are the phone numbers and locations of different sports events.

Horse Races

Horse races are held at Longchamp and Auteuil racetracks on weekends. Both tracks are located in the Bois de Boulogne park in the 16th *arrondissement*. The French take their horse racing seriously and dress well for the occasion. Each track has a restaurant. If you're in Paris in early October, you may want to get tickets for the elegant *Prix de l'Arc de Triomphe* race at Longchamp.

LONGCHAMP
Phone: 42–24–13–29

AUTEUIL
Phone: 45–27–12–25

Tennis Matches

The Roland Garros Stadium, on the western periphery of Paris, plays host to the French Open, an international tennis tournament held for two weeks, from the last few days of May through the beginning of June. I'm told that the seats sell out months in advance, but you may be able to get a ticket for the first few days of the tournament.

ROLAND GARROS
2 Avenue Gordon-Benett
Phone: 47–43–48–00
16th *arrondissement*
Métro: Porte d'Auteuil
Cost: 260 francs ($52) per seat

Team Sports

The Palais Omnisports de Paris Bercy is a large indoor stadium that plays host to many team sports, including soccer and basketball. Soccer games are also held at the Parc des Princes.

PALAIS OMNISPORTS
8 Boulevard de Bercy
Phone: 43–46–12–21
12th *arrondissement*
Métro: Bercy

PARC DES PRINCES
Avenue du Parc des Princes
Phone: 42–88–02–76
16th *arrondissement*
Métro: Pont de St.-Cloud

ENGAGING IN YOUR FAVORITE SPORT
Walking and Jogging

You will probably be doing a lot of walking, because it's the easiest and most enjoyable way to see Paris. Virtually any route you take will be charming. The most picturesque gardens and parks are listed at the end of this chapter, on pages 137–139.

Jogging is becoming more popular in Paris, although it is still limited to certain parks and to paths along the Seine River. You won't have the spectacle we have in the States of joggers running down busy boulevards at the height of rush-hour traffic inhaling the fumes. The French tend to be more "correct" about such things.

Exercise Clubs

Out of the dozens of *gymnasiums* in Paris, here are two of the best. Most emulate American methods and use Nautilus equipment.

GARDEN GYM

Garden Gym also has clubs in Palais Royal and Saint-Germain-des-Prés.

26 Rue de Berri
Phone: 43–59–04–58
8th *arrondissement*
Métro: George-V
Cards: MC, V
Cost: 100 francs ($20)
per visit

GYMNASE CLUB LES CHAMPS   ♥

This is one of the oldest and most chic clubs in Paris. The five levels offer aerobics classes (some with American instructors and music), exercise equipment, and a health-food bar on the top floor.

55 Bis, Rue de Ponthieu
Phone: 45–62–99–76
8th *arrondissement*
Métro: Franklin-D.-
Roosevelt
Credit Cards: MC, V
Cost: 130 francs ($26)
per visit

Swimming

In the summertime, Paris' pools offer a cool respite from the high temperatures. Many buildings aren't air-conditioned, so the pools become quite crowded—great for mixing with other sun-bathers and striking up new acquaintances.

AQUABOULEVARD

This is part of a chain of Forest Hills clubs located on the periphery of Paris. This club has many facilities, but some aren't available for one-time visitors.

4 Rue Louis-Armand
Phone: 40–60–10–00
15th *arrondissement*
Métro: Balard
Cost: 68 francs ($14)
for half a day at the
pool only

DELIGNY

For 150 years, Deligny's 50-meter outdoor pool has rested alongside the Seine River. This is the pool to visit in Paris. Even though the water isn't heated, the crowds are very hot. It's open from May through September.

5 Quai Anatole-France
Phone: 45–51–72–15
7th *arrondissement*
Métro: Chambre des
Députés

The Deligny Swimming Pool.

Tennis

Most of the tennis courts in Paris are private, but there is one gorgeous group of courts open to the public at the Luxembourg Gardens.

LUXEMBOURG GARDENS   ♥

The six courts are open year-round during the day. They don't accept reservations, but operate on a first-come–first-serve basis; you wait for the next available court. The surroundings are idyllic, with lots of trees, and the Luxembourg Gardens and pond are a short distance away.

Rue Guynemer
6th *arrondissement*
Métro: Luxembourg
Cost: 15 francs ($3) for
30 minutes

Bicycling

Bicycles, known as *vélos*, are a wonderful way to get some exercise while touring a park or exploring new surroundings. For the deposit, or *chèque de caution*, you can use a credit card. Generally, bicycles are rented, *louées*, for a half day or full day. The rates vary, depending on the type of bicycle and length of time, but generally run 20 francs per hour and 100 francs per day.

BICYCLUB
In Bois de Boulogne
  on Route de Suresnes
Phone: 45–20–60–33
16th *arrondissement*
Open: Saturday, Sunday, Wednesday
  9:00 A.M.–7:00 P.M.

PARIS VELO
2 Rue du Fer-à-Moulin
Phone: 43–37–59–22
5th *arrondissement*
Métro: Censier–Daubenton
Open: Monday–Saturday

Bicycles for Rent.

GARDENS AND PARKS

One reason visitors are struck by the beauty and elegance of Paris is that the city has so many lovely, well-groomed gardens and parks. These areas serve as extended living rooms where Parisians go to visit with friends, soak up the natural surroundings, and become rejuvenated. I strongly recommend that you take time out to enjoy a few hours in one of these spectacular settings. I guarantee it will be one of the highlights of your trip.

"As Post-Impressionistic French painter Georges Seurat illustrated a century ago, there is nothing better than a day in the park for a relaxed, intimate portrait of Paris and its people."
—*Sam Hall Kaplan Los Angeles Times*

Gardens

What distinguishes these gardens from the parks is that they are smaller and located in the heart of the city. The parks stretch for miles and are on the periphery of Paris. All these *jardins* are excellent for strolling, enjoying a picnic, having a *tête-à-tête* (meaning "head-to-head," or conversation) with your loved one, or curling up with a good book.

Jardin du Luxembourg.

JARDIN DU LUXEMBOURG ♥

6th *arrondissement*
Métro: Luxembourg

Located in the heart of Saint-Germain-des-Prés, this oasis is my top choice for a few hours' respite from the bustle of the city. The Luxembourg Palace, located at one end, was built in the seventeenth century for Queen Marie de Medici and now houses the French Senate. It is set off by a large pond with a fountain. The well-manicured gardens are surrounded by a densely wooded forest, with benches and sculpture sprinkled throughout. A small café, which serves drinks and light snacks, has tables on a terrace overlooking the pond.

JARDIN DU PALAIS ROYAL ♥

1st *arrondissement*
Métro: Palais-Royal

Palais Royal, commissioned by Cardinal Richelieu in the seventeenth century, is steeped in history and intrigue. Originally, the elegant apartments housed members of the royal court. The area fell into disrepute in the 1800s, when it became overrun with gambling halls and brothels, and legend has it that the French Revolution began on the steps of Rue Montpensier.

A Sculpture in the Jardin ▼
du Palais Royal.

Today, the Palais Royal gardens, fountain, and arcade have been restored to their former grace. There are two cafés with outdoor tables off Rue Montpensier, and both serve afternoon tea. Le Grand Véfour, a formal restaurant that has been a Paris landmark for decades, is at the far end of the gardens, next to Rue de Beaujolais (see details on page 92).

JARDINS DES TUILERIES

1st *arrondissement*
Métro: Tuileries

The Tuileries Gardens, built for Louis XIV, are located adjacent to the Louvre, which was the king's residence. The landscape artist, André Le Nôtre, also designed the grounds for Versailles. The gardens are just across the street from my favorite tea salon, Angelina (see page 55).

Parks

Two large parks, Bois de Boulogne and Bois de Vincennes, frame Paris on opposite ends. *Bois* means "woods," and both of these parks have miles of forest with paths for strolling and bicycling, chateaux from former royal hunting days, flower gardens, and benches for picnics.

BOIS DE BOULOGNE ♥

16th *arrondissement*
Métro: Porte Maillot or
Porte d'Auteuil

The Bois de Boulogne has lakes, gardens, restaurants, a place to rent bicycles, and a children's amusement park. One of the loveliest spots is Park Bagatelle with its formal rose gardens, manicured lawns, shimmering lakes, and a café surrounded by oak trees (Les Jardins de Bagatelle, described on page 97).

BOIS DE VINCENNES

12th *arrondissement*
Métro: St.-Mandé-
Tourelle or Porte
Dorée

Vincennes was given to the city by Napoleon III in 1860. It has a floral garden, a zoological park, and a large lake. The chateau was originally a medieval fortress.

Boat Tours: A Different Vantage Point

Boat tours along the Seine River provide a wonderful way to get out in the fresh air, soak up some sun, and enjoy a scenic view of Paris' striking monuments. This won't require much physical exertion but will definitely leave you feeling invigorated.

LES BATEAUX-MOUCHES

Would you believe *mouche* means "fly"? Don't ask me where that name came from. The fleet of boats traverses the Seine day and night, and the 90-minute ride gives you a great view of Paris and Ile Saint-Louis from the heart of the city. I don't recommend their rides with meals; they're too touristy.

Phone: 42–25–96–10
8th *arrondissement*
Métro: Alma-
   Marceau
(Walk down ramp
   next to the bridge
   on the Right Bank)
Cost: 30 francs ($6)
   per ride
Open: Seven days a
   week

LES VEDETTES DU PONT-NEUF

These boats are smaller—and thus more intimate—than the Bateaux-Mouches. Meals are not served, and the ride lasts one hour.

Phone: 46–33–98–38
1st *arrondissement*
Métro: Pont-Neuf
(You embark from
   the point of the
   island Ile de la
   Cité)
Cost: 35 francs ($7)
   per ride

Paris boasts world-famous sporting events, well-equipped health clubs, and some of the most beautiful parks in the world—countless opportunities to unwind and relax. Whether you shape up with the French at one of the *gymnasiums*, observe a tennis match at Roland Garros Stadium, or just spend an afternoon in one of the breathtaking gardens, this is bound to be an exhilarating change of pace from sightseeing and shopping.

The Bateaux-Mouches.

Diana's Fountain at Fontainebleau.

10. Les Promenades

Journey Into the Countryside

The French countryside surrounding Paris offers a tempting getaway. Here, you can escape from the bustle of the city and idle away a few hours with a loved one or friend. You will glimpse a different France and be much the wiser for the experience.

When the train pulls away from Paris, lush green fields unfold before your eyes. It's as if you are being transported back to a time when kings and queens ruled the land. Many royal retreats remain intact and are open to visitors—a testament to an era of luxury, elegance, and grace that has not been forgotten.

One of the wonderful things about Paris is that so many interesting and beautiful places exist just a short drive from the city. You can tour the wine cellars in champagne country and dine on gourmet cuisine; explore the chateaux and castles of Chantilly, Fontainebleau, and Vaux-le-Vicomte; stroll through the gardens of Giverny, the town that inspired some of Claude Monet's best-known paintings; visit Honfleur, a fishing village made world-famous by the impressionist painters who congregated there; or journey to the palace and mansions of Versailles. When possible, I've suggested restaurants and hotels in the vicinity of each listing. For information on travel by train, see page 151. My favorite choices are indicated with a heart ♥ rating.

The Art of Making Champagne

The Benedictine monk Dom Perignon discovered and developed the secrets of making champagne at the end of the seventeenth century at the Abbey of Hautvillers near Epernay. For many years, the supply of champagne was so scarce and the cost so high that the sparkling wine was available only to royalty and the very rich. Today, we are all able to celebrate in style. Here is how champagne is made.

- Late in September, the grapes are harvested and taken in baskets to the press-house, where they are emptied into large winepresses.
- After the pressing, the juice runs into vats for the *débourbage*, where any extraneous substances and particles are removed. The juice is then transferred to giant vats, where it is fermented and becomes wine.
- When the first fermentation is over, the *chef de cave* prepares the *cuvée*, a blend of various wines, to give a balanced, consistent quality to the champagne.
- In the spring, the *cuvée* is bottled and taken below to the cellars for a second fermentation, during which the wine becomes effervescent.
- At the end of the second fermentation, the bottles are placed neck-downwards, and *remueurs* turn them slightly each day for three months to coax the sediment down to the cork. A *remueur's* special training takes years, and he turns 40,000 bottles a day.
- After years of aging, the bottles are uncorked to allow for the disposal of the remaining sediment, and a liqueur mixture is added. According to the amount of liqueur added, the champagne is half-dry, dry, extra-dry, or Brut.

Champagne Country

A day in champagne country is my idea of heaven on earth. The history and culture surrounding this elixir of life are fascinating, and it's so much fun to sample the product—especially when it accompanies a gourmet meal. There are two cities in the champagne region, Epernay and Reims. Both are easily accessible by train from Gare de l'Est in Paris. Trains leave every few hours, and the ride takes a little over sixty minutes (the cost is about $20 round-trip).

Moët & Chandon, the largest champagne house in the world, is located on Avenue de Champagne in Epernay, a five-minute cab ride from the train station. The buildings, originally home to the Moët family, fill a city block.

When you arrive, you'll be greeted at the reception desk and grouped with other visitors for an underground tour of the cellars, or *caves,* conducted by an English-speaking guide. During an intriguing hour, you'll observe first-hand the dimly lit, cool, cavernous rooms where experts oversee the three-to-seven-year process of making champagne. Moët's cellars stretch for twenty miles! After the tour, you'll be invited to a complimentary tasting, or *dégustation.*

Just a few miles away from the Moët cellars (ten minutes by cab) is the Royal Champagne, one of the best restaurants and hotels in the region, and a member of the prestigious Relais & Châteaux chain. Set atop a hill over-looking grape vineyards that stretch as far as the eye can see, the Royal Champagne resembles a charming country manor. This is the perfect spot for a late lunch. The dining room is formal and gracious, and the food is gourmet.

MOET & CHANDON ♥
20 Avenue de Champagne
Phone: 26/54–71–11

ROYAL CHAMPAGNE ♥
51160 Champillon-Bellevue
Phone: 26/52–87–11
Cards: AE, MC, V
Cost: 800–1,500 francs ($160–$300)
for double room

The Cellars of Moët and Chandon.

Chantilly

You don't have to travel far to enjoy two adjoining castles with beautifully landscaped grounds and a lake. Chantilly is just north of Paris, and is reached by taking a train from Gare du Nord. Highlights include a collection of paintings by Raphael and Titian, antique jewels, and elaborate horse stables.

Fontainebleau

Starting in the twelfth century, French kings and their courts made Fontainebleau their home. Although not as grand as Versailles, Fontainebleau is viewed by the French as equally important historically. In fact, Napoleon abdicated his crown here.

Elegant and ornate, Fontainebleau is surrounded by beautiful gardens and a forest. Most important, it is not nearly as crowded as Versailles. Trains depart from Gare de Lyon for the thirty-minute ride to Avon. My favorite mode of transport from the Avon station to Fontainebleau, two miles away, is bicycle. (*Vélos*, bicycles, can be rented from many train stations.) The bicycle paths through the adjacent forest are *très romantique*.

Once inside this country palace, the tour guide will take you through the private apartments (Napoleon held a Pope prisoner in one of these for two years), drawing rooms, bed chambers, throne room, chapel, theater, and ballroom—a testament to a very luxurious, pampered lifestyle.

Bicyclists at Fontainebleau.

Claude Monet's House at Giverny.

Giverny ♥

Through his paintings, Claude Monet portrayed the French gentry of his day as they enjoyed their countryside. He is widely acclaimed for his masterful ability to create an "impression" of a scene through his use of colors and depiction of light.

In 1883, Monet moved his family to Giverny, north of Paris, and lived and worked there for over forty years, until his death. Monet went one step further than many of his colleagues by creating the setting that he painted. In *Monet's Years at Giverny*, Philippe de Montebello writes:

> The paintings immortalize the actual garden, which was the tour de force of the master gardener Monet, who planned every aspect of it. . . . There is no more happenstance in the arrangement of the flower beds, garden paths, lily pond and footbridge than there is in the many striking color juxtapositions and broad brushstrokes in the late canvases that depict them.

The gardens and main house with adjoining studio have been restored, and are open to guests April through October. The colors are stunning. The exterior of the house is salmon pink, with green doors and shutters.

The dining room is in different shades of yellow, and the kitchen sparkles in blue and white, with lots of copper touches. Monet was an avid collector of Japanese engravings, and they are displayed throughout the house.

The gardens stretch over many acres and encompass the water lily pond and Japanese footbridge that were the focus of Monet's later paintings. The flower beds near the house are laid out in rows divided by walking paths, and small nameplates describe each variety.

The gift shop carries an extensive selection of books, posters, desk items, children's puzzles, cassettes, and more. One small word of warning—film costs $20 a roll, so you should stock up beforehand. The adjacent café is rather touristy, but there is a good restaurant a block away on the main highway. Called Les Jardins de Giverny (Phone: 32/21–60–80), the restaurant takes all credit cards and has a *prix fixe* menu for 120 francs ($24).

To get to Giverny from Paris by tour bus costs approximately 260 francs ($52). (See page 34 for information on bus tours.) The more adventurous do-it-yourself types can catch a train from Gare St.-Lazare to Vernon (on the Rouen line) that takes fifty minutes; round-trip fare is about 100 francs ($20). At Vernon, there are cabs to take you the three miles to Giverny. Giverny is on the Autoroute de l'Ouest, and the phone number is 32/51–28–21. It is closed on Mondays and in the winter months.

The Lily Pond at Giverny.

Honfleur

A visit to Honfleur can be a long day trip; or, better yet, you can spend the night at one of the charming local inns and return the following day. The train ride from Gare St.-Lazare to Deauville takes two hours. Then you catch a bus or taxi to Honfleur on the *Côte de Grâce* (Coast of Grace).

The most celebrated of Honfleur's four harbors, Vieux Bassin, is flanked by seventeenth century houses. Many of the quaint shops are found between Rue de la Ville and Rue de la Prison. Musée Municipal Eugène Boudin, built to honor Honfleur native Boudin, displays his works as well as many paintings of his fellow impressionists.

Ferme Saint-Siméon, a first class hotel and restaurant associated with the prestigious Relais & Châteaux chain, is a few miles out of town on the coast. In the last century, this was the gathering place for Boudin and other impressionists while they were immortalizing Honfleur's special beauty. The hotel is in a beautiful location overlooking the sea. Filled with period antiques and surrounded by gardens, it resembles an enchanting farmhouse. The restaurant serves delicious seafood specialties and offers *prix fixe* menus weekdays at lunch time.

The following list provides information on Ferme Saint-Siméon, two other picturesque hotels, and Musée Eugène Boudin.

"Nothing really prepares you for the striking beauty, caressing light and rustic charm of this 11th-century fishing village on the Seine estuary. . . . Our first awareness of Honfleur's quaint timbered houses and sloping cobbled streets was in a Monet painting. We hardly expected to find the same scene upon arrival, but we found fifty like it."
—Beverly Beyer and Ed Rabey
Los Angeles Times

FERME SAINT-SIMEON HOTEL ♥

There are thirty-seven rooms varying in degrees of luxury, including a suite with Jacuzzi overlooking the ocean. Prices start at 1,180 francs for a double room. The restaurant is gourmet and expensive. The hotel also has a less formal restaurant, Le Manoir, a few hundred yards down the road in a lovely park.

Rue Adolphe-Marais
(Located off the coast highway west of Honfleur towards Deauville)
Phone: 31/89–23–61
Cards: MC, V

HOSTELLERIE LECHAT

This is a moderate-price hotel in a great location in the center of town. The twenty-four rooms are rustic and charming and start at 300 francs. The dining room has an outdoor terrace with tables overlooking Place Sainte-Catherine.

Place Sainte-Catherine
Phone: 31/89–23–85
Cards: AE, MC, V

HOTEL L'ECRIN

This is way off the beaten track, which adds to its intimacy. The formal decor in the twenty rooms is accented with French antiques and lush velvets. A double room starts at 340 francs and goes up to 520 francs. Breakfast is served on the veranda, but there is no restaurant for other meals.

19 Rue Eugène Boudin
Phone: 31/89–32–39
Cards: AE, MC, V

MUSEE MUNICIPAL EUGENE BOUDIN

Although the museum focuses on Eugène Boudin, there is also a collection of works by other painters who congregated in Honfleur, including Claude Monet and Alfred Sisley.

Place Erik Satie
Phone: 31/89–16–47

Vaux-Le-Vicomte

According to Robert S. Kane in *France at Its Best*, Vaux-le-Vicomte "is the French country house at its pinnacle: grand in scale but not so large that it is dizzying to comprehend; brilliant in decor but never overtly so; splendidly sited—set off by gardens at once formal and capacious—but not so extensive that they create a feeling of isolation; and, most important, stylish, elegant, and—to this very day—livable."

Nicolas Fouquet built this chateau in the 1600s after becoming King Louis XIV's minister of finance. The design and execution were so extraordinary for the time that Louis XIV decided to surpass his minister by building Versailles, and hired the same architect and designers. Fouquet's landscapist, André Le Nôtre, created beautiful gardens that are ideal for a picnic or stroll.

Vaux-le-Vicomte is thirty miles southeast of Paris and can be reached by train from Gare de Lyon.

Using the French Railroad

The French railroad, or Société Nationale de Chemins de Fer Français (S.N.C.F.), is the best in Europe. The cars are neat, clean, and comfortable, and the trains run on time. To purchase tickets, you can go to any travel agency in Paris that has the S.N.C.F. sign posted outside; or, you can buy the ticket at the station before your train departs—but be sure to allow plenty of extra time.

Paris has six different train stations, each serving a different geographical region:

The East
Gare de l'Est
Phone: 42–08–96–31

The West
Gare Montparnasse
Phone: 40–48–10–00

The South and Southeast
Gare de Lyon
Phone: 40–19–60–00

The North
Gare du Nord
Phone: 42–80–63–63

The Southwest
Gare d'Austerlitz
Phone: 45–84–14–18

The Northwest
Gare St. Lazare
Phone: 42–85–88–00

The phone number for train information on all the stations is 45–82–50–50.

An Important Regulation

Before boarding the train, you must validate your ticket by punching it in one of the orange machines placed before the *quais* (tracks) where the trains pull up (just follow all the French passengers). If you don't do this, the conductor can charge you the price of another ticket.

French Terms

When using the French railroad, you may come across signs containing a number of unfamiliar terms. The following are those most commonly used in railway stations and on the trains.

Première Classe	First Class	*Fumeur*	Smoking
Deuxième Classe	Second Class	*Non-Fumeur*	Nonsmoking
Banlieue	Suburbs (trains going nearby)	*Voiture*	Car
Grandes Lignes	Big Lines (long-distance routes)	*Potable*	Drinkable (for water in bathroom)
Quai	Track	*Non-potable*	Nondrinkable

Versailles

Versailles is both beautiful and enormous. Because of the size, you'll definitely want to wear comfortable walking shoes, and you should be prepared for crowds. The best time to go is during the week.

A half-century in the making, Versailles became the center of French society when King Louis XIV moved in with his family. They were joined by a thousand members of his court. In addition to the large Palace of Versailles, there are two smaller mansions: the Grand and Petit Trianons. The whole complex is set off by fountains, sculpture, and vast gardens that stretch as far as the eye can see. It is awesome.

Highlights in the palace include the *Galerie des Glaces*, or Hall of Mirrors, where the World War I peace treaty was signed; the *Chapelle Royale*, or Royal Chapel, where the king worshipped; and a museum with paintings depicting the history of France in the last few centuries.

The tour bus companies mentioned on page 34 offer various guided tours of Versailles, with costs ranging from 135 francs to 280 francs ($27 to $56).

If you're in Paris for more than a few days, I strongly recommend taking a short excursion into the countryside. The sights are fascinating and beautiful, and the surrounding grounds are very relaxing. This is guaranteed to be one of the highlights of your trip!

11. Les Souvenirs

Preserve Your Memories

As Ernest Hemingway so aptly stated, "Paris is a moveable feast." Once you've experienced Paris' charms, she will enhance and enlighten the rest of your life. You will return to the States with your lasting memories and with a new outlook that may change you in subtle, but profound, ways.

- You may seek out sidewalk cafés or afternoon tea salons for a *tête-à-tête* with a close friend.
- When you go to the local French restaurant, you will understand some of the items on the menu and enjoy ordering a favorite dish.
- When you wear those extra-sheer stockings, you'll feel feminine and attractive.
- When you receive compliments on your perfume, you might reply, "That's my *griffe*" (your new "signature"). You might also luxuriate in bath gel, soap, and body lotion in the same scent to create an ongoing harmony.
- You may become a regular at the nearby beauty salon for a manicure and pedicure, facial, eyelash tint, or some other luxurious treatment.
- You may spend more time in the accessory section of your department store selecting scarves, belts, and fun jewelry to accentuate your "look."
- When special exhibits come to your local museum, you will regard some of the paintings as old friends, because you saw them first in their permanent collection in Paris.
- When a debonair man extends a compliment and gazes admiringly, you will accept it in stride as a natural, welcome occurrence—one to which you've grown accustomed.

This chapter discusses how you can preserve and capture your fabulous experiences and share them with friends back home. You'll learn about taking photographs, collecting memorabilia, keeping a journal, sending postcards, and buying presents.

153

Taking Photographs

Taking photographs is a great way to preserve your memories for years to come. I prefer photographing the people and places that make Paris special for me—the view from my hotel window, the waiter at the nearby café who serves my croissant and *café au lait* each morning, or the display in the lingerie store where I bought those sexy unmentionables. Best of all, I enjoy taking pictures of and with my newly made French friends. I keep one set of photos for my scrapbook and send copies to my friends.

I recommend taking an inexpensive, lightweight camera. Theft is all too common, so it's best not to risk losing expensive equipment. And, you don't want to add more weight than necessary to the items you'll already be carrying in your purse.

Collecting Memorabilia

Paris' treasures are boundless. My house and office are full of souvenirs from previous trips, so I'm constantly reminded of wonderful times. An ashtray from Closerie des Lilas, the restaurant Hemingway frequented, is now a soap dish in my bathroom. Two signed posters from art galleries on Avenue Matignon adorn a wall in my office. Matches from an afternoon tea at the Ritz Hotel are in my kitchen. Charles Aznavour's *chansons* (songs) play on the tape deck in my car.

Most of the memorabilia I collect are inexpensive, but these items have a value far beyond their cost in francs. At museums, I buy the small paperback museum book, a few postcards, and a poster of one of the paintings. In restaurants, I collect the matchbooks and ask if I may keep a copy of the menu and buy the imprinted ashtray. There are many beautiful souvenirs sold on the streets—from old books in stands along the Seine River to young artists' watercolors displayed on streets in warm weather. The areas frequented by the sidewalk artists include the Boulevard St.-Germain; the bridges to Ile Saint-Louis; the street in front of the Louvre; and, in Montmartre, the area near Sacré-Coeur. At many of these places, you can also have your portrait drawn on the spot.

Prints for Sale on the Seine.

Keeping a Journal

Your trip to Paris will be a unique experience to savor for years to come. There are many ways to preserve the memories. My journal became the starting point for this book. Whenever I have a few minutes—sitting in a café or waiting in line—I jot down my impressions, feelings, encounters, and favorite haunts. I also collect the *carte de la maison*, or business card, of each place I visit and want to share with others.

You might put your photos and souvenirs in a scrapbook, or you might sketch your impressions, adding descriptive or poetic captions. However you record your experiences, you can be sure that friends will come to you for advice before they take their exciting trip to the City of Lights . . . and romance.

The Bureau de Poste

Neighborhood post offices are indicated by the PTT sign. They are normally open from 8:00 A.M. to 7:00 P.M. on weekdays and from 8:00 A.M. to noon on Saturdays. Not all the windows sell stamps, so look for the one marked *timbres* (stamps). Here are some other common terms that you may want to know:

Cartes postales	Postcards
Aux Etats Unis	To the United States
Par avion	Air mail
Une lettre	A letter (which requires more postage than a postcard)
A l'étranger	To foreign destinations

As of this writing, it costs 3.6 francs to send a postcard to the United States. There are two post offices that are open all the time:

52 Rue du Louvre	71 Avenue des Champs-Elysées
1st *arrondissement*	8th *arrondissement*
Métro: Louvre	Métro: George-V

These post offices also have facilities for making long-distance phone calls at a less expensive rate than that charged by hotels.

Sending Postcards

We all like to receive postcards from friends in distant lands. I also use postcards as a way of saying hello to business contacts, and the *pièce de résistance* is that I send postcards to my three cats back home (they especially love the postcards of French cats).

Cartes postales, as they are called in French, are sold at most newsstands. You can also buy postcard reproductions of paintings in the museum gift shops. Here are two stores that have big selections.

CARTES D'ART ♥

This shop has Carlos Spaventa's collection of romantic *cartes postales*. Spaventa is an American photographer based in Paris. He also took the cover photo for this guide.

9 Rue du Dragon
Phone: 42–22–86–15
6th *arrondissement*
Métro: St.-Germain-
des-Prés

A L'IMAGE DU GRENIER SUR L'EAU

In addition to postcards, this store carries posters and old newspapers.

45 Rue des
Francs-Bourgeois
Phone: 42–71–02–31
4th *arrondissement*
Métro: St.-Paul

You will also find old postcards in the *bouquinistes*, the bookstalls lining both sides of the Seine River near Notre Dame. Galeries Lafayette (see page 112) has a small counter with antique *cartes postales*. Or, you might want to try the *Marché aux Timbres* (stamp market) in the Cours Marigny near Avenue Gabriel, one block north of the Champs-Elysées (Métro: Franklin-D.-Roosevelt or Champs-Elysées-Clémenceau).

The Post Office.

Buying Presents

Small gifts—especially those that are distinctly French in flavor—make wonderful mementos to bring home to friends and family. I look for fun, simple, lightweight items that I might not readily find in the States: posters and original sketches, T-shirts and other Paris souvenirs, French perfume, colorful silk scarves, and feminine bath items.

Duty-free shops are one place to look for presents. They are located in many tourist areas, especially near the Opéra and on Rue de Rivoli, adjacent to the Tuileries Gardens (see page 53). You'll find a large selection of perfumes and soaps, ties and scarves, and other gift items for men and women. The prices are normally discounted at least 15 percent, because tax is not charged. You'll need your passport to prove you're visiting from another country. Since the *détaxe* has already been deducted, you won't have to process any forms at the airport.

When hunting for special gifts for that certain someone on your list, you can look beyond the duty-free shops to individual boutiques. While many stores in Paris offer wonderful and unusual gift items, the 6th *arrondissement* is a mecca for shoppers in search of artistic, charming gift shops. Here are a few of my favorite haunts for finding unique, reasonably priced *cadeaux* for family and friends.

GIFT BOUTIQUES

AU CHAT DORMANT ♥

The name means "sleeping cat," and cat lovers will have a field day. Everything has a cat design, and the items range from large (framed paintings and room screens) to small (trays, pillows, note pads, and cards). Of course, there is a big selection of ceramic and wooden cats.

13 Rue du Cherche-Midi
Phone: 45–49–48–63
Métro: Rennes
Cards: MC, V

GRAIN DE BEAUTE ♥

A breath of the French countryside is captured here in unusual scented objects for the house: wands of lavender woven with ribbons, pine cones scented with roses, large bunches of rosebuds fastened with velvet, and many varieties of sachets and scented papers.

9 Rue du Cherche-Midi
Phone: 45–48–07–55
Métro: Rennes
Cards: MC, V

Grain de Beauté.

NOBILIS ♥

The small, beautiful selection of scarves carried by Nobilis is not found in other stores. This shop also sells elegant leather items—wallets, eyeglass cases, and briefcases.

29 Rue Bonaparte
Phone: 43–29–21–50
Métro: St.-Germain-
des-Prés
Cards: AE, MC, V

LA ROSE DES VENTS

A potpourri of soaps, oils, and bath products from Provence are displayed, along with desk items like note pads and address books.

65 Rue de Seine
Phone: 43–26–31–46
Métro: St.-Germain-
des-Prés
Cards: MC, V

LE SAPONIFERE

In addition to expensive, exclusive scents, Le Saponifère carries bath products, shaving articles, and a big selection of makeup brushes and mirrors.

59 Rue Bonaparte
Phone: 46–33–98–43
Métro: St.-Germain-
des-Prés
Cards: MC, V

SORELLE ART DECO

This tiny shop is overflowing with antique jewelry and one-of-a-kind *objets* like perfume *flacons*—just what you would imagine finding in your grandmother's attic.

12 Rue de l'Echaudé
Phone: 46–33–59–41
Métro: St.-Germain-des-Prés
Cards: None

SUR LA PLACE   ♥

Madame Micheline Peyrot, the proprietor, is charming and speaks fluent English. She travels throughout France seeking out artisans who make hand-crafted pieces, like wooden atomizers carved from precious woods. She also offers exotic scents: Molinara from Grasse, France and Sandalwood from Mysore, India.

12 Place St.-Sulpice
Phone: 43–54–93–06
Métro: St.-Sulpice
Cards: AE, MC, V

Your photos, souvenirs, and journal entries will help keep your memories alive and allow you to share them with others. In the course of your trip, you may also be fortunate enough to make new friends. Many of my French friends have come to visit me in the States and have welcomed me into their homes in France. We stay in close touch through notes and calls, and these men and women have added a special, new dimension to my life.

From the moment you start your preparations, Paris is an enchanting dream—one that will last a lifetime. I hope this guide helps chart the course for your magical adventure.

Bon voyage!

Glossary

This glossary includes most of the French terms used throughout the guide, as well as some additional terms that may prove useful during your stay in Paris. The glossary has been organized into the following sections:

GENERAL TERMS AND PHRASES
- Conversational Phrases
- Common Terms
- Days of the Week
- Months of the Year
- Numbers

BUILDING TERMS

FOOD TERMS
- General Food Terms
- Café Terms
- Restaurant Phrases
- Menu Terms

POST OFFICE TERMS
AND PHRASES

RECREATION TERMS

ROMANTIC PHRASES

SALON TERMS
- General Salon Terms
- Beauty Salon Terms
- Hair Salon Terms

SHOPPING PHRASES AND TERMS
- Shopping Phrases
- General Shopping Terms
- Clothing Terms

TRANSPORTATION TERMS
- Métro Terms
- Train Terms

Each section starts with an alphabetical listing of the English words, along with the French translations. In most cases this is followed by the French/English version.

Bonne chance! Translation: Good luck!

GENERAL TERMS AND PHRASES
Conversational Phrases

English/French

Do you speak English? *Parlez-vous anglais?*
Excuse me. *Excusez-moi.*
Good-bye. *Au revoir.*
Hello. *Bonjour.*
How are you? *Comment allez-vous?*
How do you say _____ in French? *Comment dit-on _____ en français?*
Madame. *Madame.*
My name is _____. *Je m'appelle _____ .*
No. *Non.*
Please. *S'il vous plaît.*
Sir. *Monsieur.*
Thank you. *Merci.*
Very well, thanks. And you? *Très bien, merci. Et vous?*
What's your name? *Comment-vous appelez-vous?*
Yes. *Oui.*
You're welcome. *Je vous en prie.*

French/English

Au revoir. Good-bye.
Bonjour. Hello.
Comment allez-vous? How are you?
Comment dit-on _____ en français? How do you say _____ in French?
Comment-vous appelez-vous? What's your name?
Excusez-moi. Excuse me.
Je m'appelle _____ . My name is _____ .
Je vous en prie. You're welcome.
Madame. Madame.
Merci. Thank you.
Monsieur. Sir.
Non. No.
Oui. Yes.
Parlez-vous anglais? Do you speak English?
S'il vous plaît. Please.
Très bien, merci. Et vous? Very well, thanks. And you?

Common Terms

English/French

A lot. *Beaucoup.*
Bridges. *Ponts.*
Business card. *Carte de la maison*
Courtesy. *Courtoisie.*
Dry cleaners. *Nettoyage à sec.*
Eighth. *Huitième.*

French/English

Arrondissement. Neighborhood.
Beaucoup. A lot.
Bien connu. Well known.
Bureaux. Offices.
Cadeaux. Gifts.
Carte de la maison. Business card.

First. *Premier.*
Forbidden. *Interdit.*
Fourth. *Quatrième.*
Gifts. *Cadeaux.*
House. *Maison.*
Kindness. *Gentillesse.*
Most popular. *Plus populaire.*
Neighborhood. *Arrondissement.*
Newsstands. *Kiosks.*
Offices. *Bureaux.*
Sixteenth. *Seizième.*
Sixth. *Sixième.*
Songs. *Chansons.*
The good life. *La belle vie.*
Very chic. *Très mode.*
Very expensive. *Très cher.*
Well known. *Bien connu.*

Chansons. Songs.
Courtoisie. Courtesy.
Gentillesse. Kindness.
Huitième. Eighth.
Interdit. Forbidden.
Kiosks. Newsstands.
La belle vie. The good life.
Maison. House.
Nettoyage à sec. Dry cleaners.
Plus populaire. Most popular.
Ponts. Bridges.
Premier. First.
Quatrième. Fourth.
Seizième. Sixteenth.
Sixième. Sixth.
Très cher. Very expensive.
Très mode. Very chic.

Days of the Week

English/French

Monday. *Lundi.*
Tuesday. *Mardi.*
Wednesday. *Mercredi.*
Thursday. *Jeudi.*
Friday. *Vendredi.*
Saturday. *Samedi.*
Sunday. *Dimanche.*

French/English

Lundi. Monday.
Mardi. Tuesday.
Mercredi. Wednesday.
Jeudi. Thursday.
Vendredi. Friday.
Samedi. Saturday.
Dimanche. Sunday.

Months of the Year

English/French

January. *Janvier.*
February. *Février.*
March. *Mars.*
April. *Avril.*
May. *Mai.*
June. *Juin.*
July. *Juillet.*

French/English

Janvier. January.
Février. February.
Mars. March.
Avril. April.
Mai. May.
Juin. June.
Juillet. July.

August. *Août.*
September. *Septembre.*
October. *Octobre.*
November. *Novembre.*
December. *Décembre.*

Août. August.
Septembre. September.
Octobre. October.
Novembre. November.
Décembre. December.

Numbers

English/French

One. *Un.*
Two. *Deux.*
Three. *Trois.*
Four. *Quatre.*
Five. *Cinq.*
Six. *Six.*
Seven. *Sept.*
Eight. *Huit.*
Nine. *Neuf.*
Ten. *Dix.*
Eleven. *Onze.*
Twelve. *Douze.*
Thirteen. *Treize.*
Fourteen. *Quatorze.*
Fifteen. *Quinze.*
Sixteen. *Seize.*
Seventeen. *Dix-sept.*
Eighteen. *Dix-huit.*
Nineteen. *Dix-neuf.*
Twenty. *Vingt.*
Thirty. *Trente.*
Forty. *Quarante.*
Fifty. *Cinquante.*

French/English

Un. One.
Deux. Two.
Trois. Three.
Quatre. Four.
Cinq. Five.
Six. Six.
Sept. Seven.
Huit. Eight.
Neuf. Nine.
Dix. Ten.
Onze. Eleven.
Douze. Twelve.
Treize. Thirteen.
Quatorze. Fourteen.
Quinze. Fifteen.
Seize. Sixteen.
Dix-sept. Seventeen.
Dix-huit. Eighteen.
Dix-neuf. Nineteen.
Vingt. Twenty
Trente. Thirty.
Quarante. Forty.
Cinquante. Fifty.

BUILDING TERMS

English/French

Bath. *Bain*
Do not enter. *Interdit.*
Elevator. *Ascenseur.*
Emergency exit. *Sortie de secours.*
Escalator. *Escalier roulant.*
Exit. *Sortie.*
Ladies (for restroom). *Dames.*
Men (for restroom). *Messieurs.*
Pull. *Tirez.*
Push. *Poussez.*
Shower. *Douche.*
Stairs. *Escaliers.*

French/English

Ascenseur. Elevator.
Bain. Bath.
Dames. Ladies (for restroom).
Douche. Shower.
Escalier roulant. Escalator.
Escaliers. Stairs.
Interdit. Do not enter.
Messieurs. Men (for restroom).
Poussez. Push.
Sortie. Exit.
Sortie de secours. Emergency exit.
Tirez. Pull.

FOOD TERMS
General Food Terms

English/French

Bakery. *Boulangerie.*
Cheese shop. *Fromagerie.*
Delicatessen with gourmet take-out foods. *Charcuterie.*
Dinner. *Dîner.*
Lunch. *Déjeuner.*
Market. *Marché.*
Meat shop. *Boucherie.*
Of the house. *De la maison.*
Pastry shop. *Pâtisserie.*
Shellfish. *Fruits de mer.*
Tasting. *Dégustation.*
Tea salon. *Salon de thé.*
Wine bars. *Bars à vins.*

French/English

A la carte. Literally, "Off the menu," with each dish ordered and priced separately.
Bars à vins. Wine bars.
Boucherie. Meat shop.
Boulangerie. Bakery.
Charcuterie. Gourmet take-out, like a delicatessen.
De la maison. Of the house.
Dégustation. Tasting.
Déjeuner. Lunch.
Dîner. Dinner.
Fromagerie. Cheese shop.
Fruits de mer. Shellfish.
Marché. Market.
Pâtisserie. Pastry shop.
Prix fixe. One price for a number of courses.
Salon de thé. Tea salon.

Café Terms

English/French

Black coffee that's very strong (or espresso). *Café noir.*
Coffee with steamed milk. *Café au lait* (or *café crème*).
Decaffeinated coffee. *Décaféiné* or *décaf.*
Drip coffee, which is less strong than other types. *Café filtre.*
Herb tea. *Infusion.*
Hot chocolate. *Chocolat chaud.*
Tea with lemon. *Thé au citron.*
Tea with milk. *Thé au lait.*
Tea without milk or lemon. *Thé nature.*

French/English

Café au lait (or *café crème*). Coffee with steamed milk.
Café filtre. Uses drip method, less strong.
Café noir. Plain, very strong black coffee (or espresso).
Chocolat chaud. Hot chocolate.
Décaféiné or *décaf.* Decaffeinated coffee.
Infusion. Herb tea.
Thé au citron. Tea with lemon.
Thé au lait. Tea with milk.
Thé nature. Plain tea.

Restaurant Phrases

English/French

Have you decided? *Avez-vous choisi?*
I would like to see the menu. *Je voudrais voir la carte.*
Service included (15 percent). *Service compris.*
The check, please. *L'addition, s'il vous plaît.*

French/English

Avez-vous choisi? Have you decided?
Je voudrais voir la carte. I would like to see the menu.
L'addition, s'il vous plaît. The check, please.
Service compris. Service included (15 percent).

Menu Terms

English/French

Apple. *Pomme.*
Artichoke. *Artichaut.*
Asparagus. *Asperge.*
Avocado. *Avocat.*

French/English

Addition. Bill.
Ananas. Pineapple.
Artichaut. Artichoke.
Asperge. Asparagus.

Beef rib steak. *Entrecôte.*
Bill; check. *Addition.*
Bread. *Pain.*
Butter. *Beurre.*
Buttery roll. *Brioche.*
Cake. *Gâteau.*
Cheese. *Fromage.*
Chicken. *Poulet.*
Coffee. *Café.*
Cold cuts. *Charcuteries.*
Dinner; to dine. *Dîner.*
Dish. *Plat.*
Drinks. *Boissons.*
Duck. *Canard.*
Egg. *Oeuf.*
First course. *Entrée.*
Fish. *Poisson.*
Grape. *Raisin.*
Grapefruit. *Pamplemousse.*
Green bean. Haricot vert.
Ham. Jambon.
Ice cream. *Glace.*
Juice. *Jus.*
Lamb chop. *Côte d'agneau.*
Lemon. *Citron.*
Lunch. *Déjeuner.*
Meat. *Viande.*
Menu. *Carte.*
Milk. *Lait.*
Mushroom. *Champignon.*
Napkin. *Serviette.*
Peach. *Pêche.*
Pepper. *Poivre.*
Pineapple. *Ananas.*
Plate. *Assiette.*
Potato. *Pomme de terre.*
Receipt. *Reçu.*
Salmon. *Saumon.*
Salt. *Sel.*
Shellfish. *Coquillages.*
Soup. *Potage.*

Assiette. Plate.
Avocat. Avocado.
Beurre. Butter.
Bifteck. Steak.
 A point. Medium.
 Bien cuit. Well done.
 Saignant. Rare.
Boissons. Drinks.
Brioche. Buttery roll.
Café. Coffee.
Canard. Duck.
Carte. Menu.
Champignon. Mushroom.
Charcuteries. Cold cuts.
Citron. Lemon.
Coquillages. Shellfish.
Côte d'agneau. Lamb chop.
Crème fraîche. Thick, sour, heavy
 cream.
Crudités. Raw vegetables.
Déjeuner. Lunch.
Dîner. Dinner; to dine.
Entrecôte. Beef rib steak.
Entrée. First course.
Fromage. Cheese.
Gâteau. Cake.
Glace. Ice cream.
Haricot vert. Green bean.
Jambon. Ham.
Jus. Juice.
Lait. Milk.
Légume. Vegetable.
Oeuf. Egg.
Pain. Bread.
Pamplemousse. Grapefruit.
Pêche. Peach.
Plat. A dish.
Poisson. Fish.
Poivre. Pepper.
Pomme. Apple.
Pomme de terre. Potato.
Potage. Soup.

Steak. *Bifteck.*
  Medium. *A point.*
  Rare. *Saignant.*
  Well done. *Bien cuit.*
Tea. *Thé.*
Tuna fish. *Thon.*
Veal. *Veau.*
Vegetable. *Légume.*

Poulet. Chicken.
Raisin. Grape.
Reçu. Receipt.
Saumon. Salmon.
Sel. Salt.
Serviette. Napkin.
Thé. Tea.
Thon. Tuna fish.
Veau. Veal.
Viande. Meat.

POST OFFICE TERMS AND PHRASES

English/French

A letter (which requires more postage than a postcard). *Une lettre.*
Air mail. *Par avion.*
Post office. *Bureau de poste.*
Postcards. *Cartes postales.*
Stamp markets. *Marché aux timbres.*
Stamps. *Timbres.*
To foreign destinations. *A l'étranger.*
To the United States. *Aux Etats Unis.*

French/English

A l'étranger. To foreign destinations.
Aux Etats Unis. To the United States.
Bureau de poste. Post office.
Cartes postales. Postcards.
Marché aux timbres. Stamp markets.
Par avion. Air mail.
Timbres. Stamps.
Une lettre. A letter (which requires more postage than a postcard).

RECREATION TERMS

English/French

Bicycle. *Vélo.*
Gardens. *Jardins.*
Health club. *Gymnasium.*
Stadium. *Stade.*
Swimming pool. *Piscine.*
Team. *Equipe.*
Woods. *Bois.*

French/English

Bois. Woods.
Equipe. Team.
Gymnasium. Health club.
Jardins. Gardens.
Piscine. Swimming pool.
Stade. Stadium.
Vélo. Bicycle.

ROMANTIC PHRASES

English/French

Flash of lightning; love at first sight. *Coup de foudre.*

Head-to-head; intimate conversation. *Tête-à-tête.*

The chase. *La chasse.*

The conquest. *La conquête.*

Very poetic. *Très poétique.*

Very romantic. *Très romantique.*

I adore you. *Je t'adore.*

I can't live without you. *Je ne peux vivre sans toi.*

I dream of you. *Je rêve de toi.*

I drink you with my eyes. *Je te bois des yeux.*

I have the desire to caress you. *J'ai envie de te caresser.*

I kiss you all over. *Je t'embrasse partout.*

I love you. *Je t'aime.*

I miss you. *Tu me manques.*

I throw myself at your feet. *Je me jette à vos pieds.*

My dear. *Mon chéri.*

My love. *Mon amour.*

The time passes slowly without you. *C'est long sans toi.*

We are made to be together. *Nous sommes faits pour nous entendre.*

You are beautiful. *Tu es belle.*

You are handsome. *Tu es beau.*

You are radiant. *Tu es rayonnante.*

You shatter my heart. *Tu me fais craquer.*

French/English

Coup de foudre. Flash of lightning; love at first sight.

La chasse. The chase.

La conquête The conquest.

Tête-a-tête. Head-to-head, intimate conversation.

Très poétique. Very poetic.

Très romantique. Very romantic.

C'est long sans toi. The time passes slowly without you.

J'ai envie de te caresser. I have the desire to caress you.

Je me jette à vos pieds. I throw myself at your feet.

Je ne peux vivre sans toi. I can't live without you.

Je t'adore. I adore you.

Je t'aime. I love you.

Je te bois des yeux. I drink you with my eyes.

Je t'embrasse partout. I kiss you all over.

Je rêve de toi. I dream of you.

Mon amour. My love.

Mon chéri. My dear.

Nous sommes faits pour nous entendre. We are made to be together.

Tu es beau. You are handsome.

Tu es belle. You are beautiful.

Tu es rayonnante. You are radiant.

Tu me fais craquer. You shatter my heart.

Tu me manques. I miss you.

SALON TERMS
General Salon Terms

English/French

Beauty salon. *Salon de beauté.*
Beauty salon professional.
  Esthéticienne.
Couture designer/owner.
  Couturière.
Hairdresser. *Coiffeur.*
Signature (a woman's perfume
  scent). *Griffe.*

French/English

Coiffeur. Hairdresser.
Couturière. Couture
  designer/owner.
Esthéticienne. Beauty salon profes-
  sional.
Griffe. Signature (a woman's per-
  fume scent).
Salon de beauté. Beauty salon.

Beauty Salon Terms

English/French

Body massage. *Modelage esthé-
tique relaxant.*
Eyelash curl. *Permanente de cils.*
Eyelash tint. *Teinture des cils.*
Facial. *Beauté complète du
visage.*
Makeup application. *Maquillage.*
Manicure. *Manucure.*
Pedicure. *La beauté des pieds.*

French/English

Beauté complète du visage. Facial.
La beauté des pieds. Pedicure.
Manucure. Manicure.
Maquillage. Makeup application.
Modelage esthétique relaxant.
  Body massage.
Permanente de cils. Eyelash curl.
Teinture des cils. Eyelash tint.

Hair Salon Terms

English/French

Blow Dry. *Brushing.*
Color. *Couleur.*
Cut. *Coupe.*
Hair. *Cheveux.*
Wash. *Shampooing.*

French/English

Brushing. Blow Dry.
Cheveux. Hair.
Couleur. Color.
Coupe. Cut.
Shampooing. Wash.

SHOPPING PHRASES AND TERMS
Shopping Phrases

English/French

Do you accept credit cards or traveler's checks? *Acceptez-vous les cartes de crédit ou les chèques de voyage?*
How much does this cost? *Ca coûte combien?*

I would like the Export Sales Invoice for sales tax reimbursement. *Je voudrais l'imprimé pour la détaxe.*
I would like the package gift wrapped. *Je voudrais un paquet cadeau.*

General Shopping Terms

English/French

Accessories. *Accessoires.*
Fake jewels; costume jewelry. *Faux bijoux.*
Flea markets. *Marchés aux puces*
High fashion. *Haute couture.*
On sale. *Soldes.*
Ready to wear. *Prêt à porter.*
Real jewels. *Vrai bijoux.*
Sales tax. *Détaxe.*

French/English

Accessoires. Accessories.
Détaxe. Sales tax.
Faux bijoux. Fake jewels; costume jewelry.
Haute couture. High fashion.
Marchés aux puces. Flea markets.
Prêt à porter. Ready to wear.
Soldes. On sale.
Vrai bijoux. Real jewels.

Clothing Terms

English/French

Belt. *Ceinture.*
Blouse. *Blouse.*
Boots. *Bottine.*
Coat. *Manteau.*
Dress. *Robe.*
Glove. *Gant.*
Nightgown. *Peignoir.*
Pants. *Pantalon.*
Scarf. *Echarpe.*
Shoes. *Chaussures.*

French/English

Bas. Stockings.
Blouse. Blouse.
Bottine. Boots.
Ceinture. Belt.
Chaussures. Shoes.
Cravate. Tie.
Echarpe. Scarf.
Gant. Glove.
Jupe. Skirt.
Manteau. Coat.

Size. *Taille.*
Skirt. *Jupe.*
Stockings. *Bas.*
Sweater. *Pullover.*
Tie. *Cravate.*

Pantalon. Pants.
Peignoir. Nightgown.
Pullover. Sweater.
Robe. Dress.
Taille. Size.

TRANSPORTATION TERMS
Métro Terms

English/French

Connecting métro lines.
  Correspondances.
Exit. *Sortie.*
One ticket. *Billet.*
Pull (on door). *Tirez.*
Punch (bus ticket). *Oblitérer.*
Push (on door). *Poussez.*
Special express métro lines that go into the suburbs and make only a few stops in Paris. *RER.*
Taxi stand. *Tête de station.*
Ten tickets. *Carnet.*

French/English

Billet. One ticket.
Carnet. Ten tickets..
Correspondances. Connecting métro lines.
Oblitérer. Punch (bus ticket).
Poussez. Push (on door).
RER. Special express métro lines that go into the suburbs and make only a few stops in Paris.
Sortie. Exit.
Tête de station. Taxi stand.
Tirez. Pull (on door).

Train Terms

English/French

Big lines (long-distance routes).
  Grandes lignes.
Car. *Voiture.*
Drinkable (for water in bathroom). *Potable.*
First Class. *Première Classe.*
Nondrinkable. *Non-potable.*
Nonsmoking. *Non-fumeur.*
Second Class. *Deuxième Classe.*
Smoking. *Fumeur.*
Suburbs (trains going nearby).
  Banlieue.
Track. *Quai.*

French/English

Banlieue. Suburbs (trains going nearby).
Deuxième Classe. Second Class.
Fumeur. Smoking.
Grandes lignes. Big lines (long-distance routes).
Non-fumeur. Nonsmoking.
Non-potable. Nondrinkable.
Potable. Drinkable (for water in bathroom).
Première Classe. First Class.
Quai. Track.
Voiture. Car.

Suggested Reading List

The following books served as valuable references during my research and writing. They are all fascinating reading and go into great depth about various aspects of French culture.

Bernstein, Richard. *Fragile Glory: A Portrait of France and the French.* Alfred A. Knopf, New York, 1990.

Richard Bernstein, correspondent for *The New York Times* in Paris from 1984 to 1987, has traveled extensively throughout France to give us a first-hand account of French life and attitudes today.

Hemingway, Ernest. *A Moveable Feast.* Charles Scribner's Sons, New York, 1964.

In 1950, Ernest Hemingway wrote to a friend, "If you are lucky enough to have lived in Paris as a young man, then wherever you go for the rest of your life, it stays with you, for Paris is a moveable feast." This book presents sketches of Hemingway's early life in Paris in the 1920s.

Russell, John. *Paris.* Harry N. Abrams, Inc., New York, 1983.

In this volume, beautifully illustrated with more than 310 paintings, pastels, drawings, and photographs, John Russell takes the reader on a tour of Paris' many neighborhoods, all the while training his highly educated eye on the French culture and its fascinating history.

Sommers, Susan. *French Chic: How to Dress Like a Frenchwoman.* Villard Books, New York, 1988.

French Chic is a wonderful primer on how French women exude an aura of femininity, sexual appeal, and high fashion—even when they're wearing jeans and a T-shirt. Sommers also gives a step-by-step explanation of how you can achieve the same result.

Steele, Valerie. *Paris Fashion: A Cultural History.* Oxford University Press, New York, 1988.

Valerie Steele looks at the preeminent position French fashion has held in the world, and explores its role as a cultural ideal and social phenomenon.

Wells, Patricia. *The Food Lover's Guide to Paris.* Workman Publishing, New York, 1988.

American Patricia Wells lives in Paris and has become one of the authoritative voices on French cuisine. This book tells all, from detailed descriptions of gourmet food shops to a thorough listing of restaurants that serve French cuisine. Many recipes are included.

Index

From the Michelin Paris Plan (1990 edition), Pneu Michelin, Services de Tourisme.

THE SIXTH ARRONDISSEMENT.

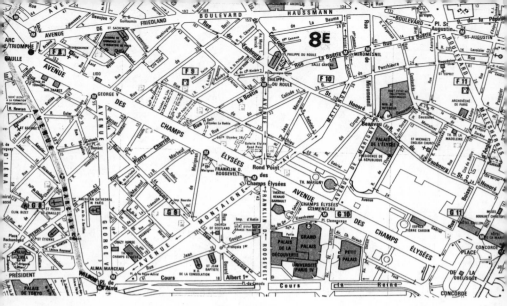

From the Michelin Paris Plan (1990 edition), Pneu Michelin, Services de Tourisme.

THE EIGHTH ARRONDISSEMENT.

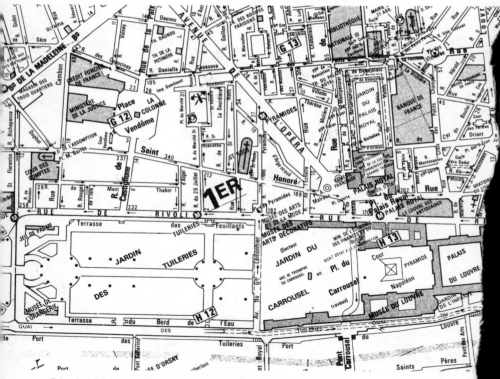

From the Michelin Paris Plan (1990 edition), Pneu Michelin, Services de Tourisme.

THE FIRST ARRONDISSEMENT.